'Diane Morgan's study on Immanuel Kant and his relevance to architectural thought and theory is a magnificent, thoughtful and provocative study of Kant's ideas about building and dwelling, but more importantly, of his notions of cosmopolitics which introduce a global perspective to the idea of building homes and worlds. Indeed, Kant's "cosmic" and holistic understanding of the world is a necessary underpinning for any theory of sustainability, ecology and the cosmopolitan spirit.'

– Professor Nicole Pohl, Editor of *Utopian Studies*, UK

'In this brief and yet eloquent introduction to the evolving relationship between Kant's critical philosophy and the theory and practice of architecture Diane Morgan demonstrates with critical verve, lucid erudition and a wide range of vivid and luminous examples from both architecture and philosophy how the Vitruvian architectural virtues of integrity, utility and aesthetic delight can apply as much to an account of the dialogue between these two disciplines as to the problems or questions encountered within them.'

– Dr. Charlie Blake, University of West London, UK

KANT FOR ARCHITECTS

This book introduces architects to a philosopher, Immanuel Kant, whose work was constantly informed by a concern for the world as an evolving whole. According to Kant, in this interconnected and dynamic world, humans should act as mutually dependent and responsible subjects. Given his future-oriented and ethico-politically concerned thinking, Kant is a thinker who clearly speaks to architects. This introduction demonstrates how his ideas bear pertinently and creatively upon the world in which we live now and for which we should care thoughtfully.

Kant grounded his enlightened vision of philosophy's mission using an architectural metaphor: of the modest 'dwelling house'. Far from constructing speculative 'castles in the sky' or vertiginous 'towers which reach to the heavens', he tells us that his humble aim is rather to build a 'secure home for ourselves', one which appropriately corresponds at once to the limited material resources available on our planet, and to our need for firm and solid principles to live by. This book also explores Kant's notions of cosmopolitics, which attempts to think politics from a global perspective by taking into account the geographical fact that the earth is a sphere with limited land mass and natural resources. Given the urgent topicality of sustainable development, these Kantian texts are of particular interest for architects today.

Students of architecture, who are necessarily trained in negotiating between theory and practice, gain much from considering Kant, whose critical project also consisted of testing and exploring the viability of ideas, so as to ascertain to what extent, and crucially, *how* ideas can have a constructive effect on the whole world, and on us as active agents therein.

Diane Morgan is Lecturer in Cultural Studies at the School of Fine Art, History of Art and Cultural Studies, University of Leeds, UK.

Thinkers for Architects

Series Editor: Adam Sharr, Newcastle University, UK

Editorial Board

Jonathan A. Hale, University of Nottingham, UK
Hilde Heynen, KU Leuven, Netherlands
David Leatherbarrow, University of Pennsylvania, USA

Architects have often looked to philosophers and theorists from beyond the discipline for design inspiration or in search of a critical framework for practice. This original series offers quick, clear introductions to key thinkers who have written about architecture and whose work can yield insights for designers.

'**Each unintimidatingly slim book makes sense of the subjects' complex theories.**'

Building Design

'... a valuable addition to any studio space or computer lab.'

Architectural Record

'... a creditable attempt to present their subjects in a useful way.'

Architectural Review

Foucault for Architects
Gordana Fontana-Giusti

Virilio for Architects
John Armitage

Goodman for Architects
Remei Capdevila-Werning

Merleau-Ponty for Architects
Jonathan Hale

Lefebvre for Architects
Nathaniel Coleman

Kant for Architects
Diane Morgan

THINKERS FOR ARCHITECTS

Kant
for
Architects

Diane Morgan

LONDON AND NEW YORK

First published 2018
by Routledge
2 Park Square, Milton Park, Abingdon, Oxon OX14 4RN

and by Routledge
711 Third Avenue, New York, NY 10017

Routledge is an imprint of the Taylor & Francis Group, an informa business

© 2018 Diane Morgan

The right of Diane Morgan to be identified as author of this work has been asserted by her in accordance with sections 77 and 78 of the Copyright, Designs and Patents Act 1988.

All rights reserved. No part of this book may be reprinted or reproduced or utilised in any form or by any electronic, mechanical, or other means, now known or hereafter invented, including photocopying and recording, or in any information storage or retrieval system, without permission in writing from the publishers.

Trademark notice: Product or corporate names may be trademarks or registered trademarks, and are used only for identification and explanation without intent to infringe.

British Library Cataloguing-in-Publication Data
A catalogue record for this book is available from the British Library

Library of Congress Cataloging-in-Publication Data
Names: Morgan, Diane, 1963– author.
Title: Kant for architects / Diane Morgan.
Description: New York : Routledge, 2017. | Series: Thinkers for architects | Includes bibliographical references and index.
Identifiers: LCCN 2017020042 | ISBN 9780415698689 (hb : alk. paper) | ISBN 9780415698696 (pb : alk. paper) | ISBN 9781315719795 (ebook)
Subjects: LCSH: Kant, Immanuel, 1724–1804. | Architecture–Philosophy.
Classification: LCC B2797 .M67 2017 | DDC 193–dc23
LC record available at https://lccn.loc.gov/2017020042

ISBN: 978-0-415-69868-9 (hbk)
ISBN: 978-0-415-69869-6 (pbk)
ISBN: 978-1-315-71979-5 (ebk)

Typeset in Frutiger
by Out of House Publishing

To Bernard, a master-builder

Contents

Series editor's preface — xi
Illustration credits — xiii
Acknowledgements — xv

Introduction: why Kant now? — 1

1. Placing Kant: the city of Königsberg/Kaliningrad — 12

2. Kant, the critical project and architecture — 24

    Does a house necessarily stand? 37
    Is a house necessarily solid and fixed? 40
    Reaching for the skies: building the tower and multivocality 42

3. The precarious situation of architecture and its relation to beauty — 48

    Architecture: too down-to-earth to be beautiful? 50
    What does beauty care about? 57
    The beautiful, the utopian dream and the 'real' world of consumer culture 59

4. From the sublime to the cosmopolitical — 95

    Measuring the sublime and its relation to architecture 97
    The sublime, nature and an expanded notion of architecture 107

5. Building cosmopolitically? 'Fluid geography' and 'total thinking' 113

    The cosmic viewpoint and architecture 114
    Tension as a constructive force 118

    Conclusion: architects of the future unite! 125

    Further reading 128
    Bibliography 130
    Index 138

Series editor's preface

Adam Sharr

Architects have often looked to thinkers in philosophy and theory for design ideas, or in search of a critical framework for practice. Yet architects and students of architecture can struggle to navigate thinkers' writings. It can be daunting to approach original texts with little appreciation of their contexts. And existing introductions seldom explore a thinker's architectural material in any detail. This original series offers clear, quick and accurate introductions to key thinkers who have written about architecture. Each book summarises what a thinker has to offer for architects. It locates their architectural thinking in the body of their work, introduces significant books and essays, helps decode terms and provides quick reference for further reading. If you find philosophical and theoretical writing about architecture difficult, or just don't know where to begin, this series will be indispensable.

Books in the *Thinkers for Architects* series come out of architecture. They pursue architectural modes of understanding, aiming to introduce a thinker to an architectural audience. Each thinker has a unique and distinctive ethos, and the structure of each book derives from the character at its focus. The thinkers explored are prodigious writers and any short introduction can only address a fraction of their work. Each author – an architect or an architectural critic – has focused on a selection of a thinker's writings which they judge most relevant to designers and interpreters of architecture. Inevitably, much will be left out. These books will be the first point of reference, rather than the last word, about a particular thinker for architects. It is hoped that they will encourage you to read further, offering an incentive to delve deeper into the original writings of a particular thinker.

The *Thinkers for Architects* series has proved highly successful, expanding to fourteen volumes dealing with familiar cultural figures whose writings have influenced architectural designers, critics and commentators in distinctive and important ways. Books explore the work of: Gilles Deleuze and Felix Guattari; Martin Heidegger; Luce Irigaray; Homi Bhabha; Pierre Bourdieu; Walter Benjamin; Jacques Derrida; Hans-Georg Gadamer, Michael Foucault, Nelson Goodman, Henri Lefebvre, Paul Virilio, Maurice Merleau-Ponty, and now Immanuel Kant. Future volumes are projected, addressing the work of Jacques Lacan and Jean Baudrillard. The series continues to expand, addressing an increasingly rich diversity of thinkers who have something to say to architects.

Adam Sharr is Head of the School of Architecture, Planning and Landscape at Newcastle University, Principal of Adam Sharr Architects and Editor-in-Chief of *arq: Architectural Research Quarterly*, a Cambridge University Press international architecture journal. His books published by Routledge include *Heidegger for Architects* and *Reading Architecture and Culture*.

Illustration credits

Acknowledgements
1. Heinrich von Kleist, Zusatz vom 30. Dezember 1800 (Project Gutenberg). xvi

2. Kant, the critical project and architecture
    2. Douiret, Tunisia (image author's own). 38
    3. Matmata, Tunisia (image author's own). 38
    4. David Greene (Suit made by Pat Haines based on the Suitaloon project by Michael Webb) © Archigram 1968. Photograph Dennis Crompton. 41
    5. Building site of La Fondation Louis Vuitton (image author's own). 44
    6. Building site of La Fondation Louis Vuitton (image author's own). 45

3. The precarious situation of architecture and its relation to beauty
    7. Exterior view of La Fondation Louis Vuitton, © Fondation Louis Vuitton/ Thomas Depin. 60
    8. Sauerbruch & Hutton's Jessop West Building, University of Sheffield 2008, ©h Noshe. 80
    9. Caryatids, rue des petites écuries, Paris 10ᵉ (image author's own). 83
    10. Santa Maria della Pietà, via Torremuzza, Palermo (image author's own). 86
    11. Francis Solers' French Ministry of Culture, Paris 2004 (image author's own). 88

4. From the sublime to the cosmopolitical
    12. Close-up of Egyptian pyramids (Wikimedia Commons). 105
    13. Giovanni Paolo Panini's 'Interior of St Peter's in Rome', 1750 (Wikimedia Commons). 106

5. Building cosmopolitically? 'Fluid geography' and 'total thinking'

14. Ara Güler 'Kumkapi fisherman returning to port in the first light of dawn', 1950, © Magnum Photos. 117
15. Buckminster Fuller holding a tensegrity mast c.1950 © Courtesy, the Estate of R. Buckminster Fuller. 119
16. Buckminster Fuller and his students testing their geodesic dome experiment at the Black Mountain College, 1949 © Courtesy, the Estate of R. Buckminster Fuller. 123

Acknowledgements

In March 1801, Kleist encountered Kantian philosophy. The consequences for him were devastating. He erroneously believed that Kant's putting into question our knowledge about things in themselves meant that all our certitudes become groundless, that all that we have experienced in the world is revealed as having been based on nothing substantial. He described himself as 'painfully shattered' by such thoughts. My experience of reading Kant does not resemble Kleist's. As I hope to demonstrate, for me he is more a thinker who encourages one to try to get a grip on the world, to act as a moral agent within it. To be sure, Kant solicits our assumptions. Nevertheless, he impresses upon us that we have the structural capacity to resist such critique, and indeed even to evolve because of it.

Before what is known as his 'Kant-crisis', and evidently before his suicide at the Kleiner Wannsee, Berlin on 21 November 1811, Kleist had rather boastfully proclaimed to his girlfriend, Wilhelmine von Zenge, that he had discovered a resourceful idea about how to resist life's trials and tribulations. He related to her that he drew his comfort from the study of architectural forms. His story runs as follows:

> On the evening before the most important day of my life, I went for a walk in Würzburg. As the sun sank it seemed to me as if my happiness was sinking with it. I shuddered to think that perhaps I must cut myself off from everything that was dear to me. Then, walking back to town deep in thought, I went through a vaulted gateway. 'Why,' I wondered, 'does the vault not cave inwards as it has no support?' 'It stands,' I replied, 'because all the stones want to collapse at once' – and out of this thought I drew to me an indescribably reassuring consolation, which has stood by my side even in the most decisive moments, that I, too, would not collapse, even if I lost all courage.

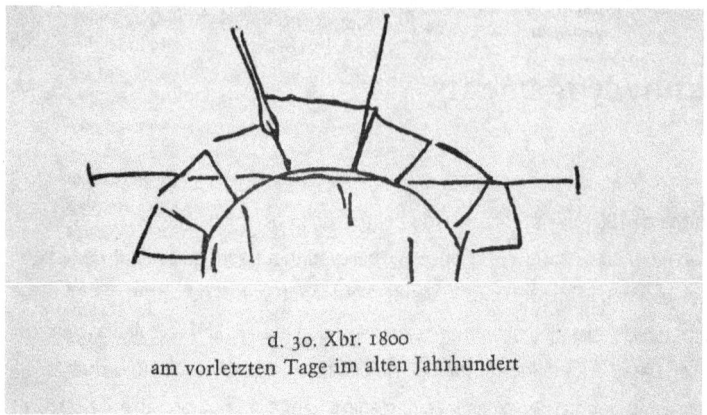

d. 30. Xbr. 1800
am vorletzten Tage im alten Jahrhundert

Kleist's addition to his letters of 16 and 18 November 1800 from 30 December. The vaulted gateway of Würzburg.

I'd like to acknowledge how my friends, as well as Bernard, Joseph and Gladys, in effect hold things in place, even *if* it feels, and especially *when*, all is about to collapse. Friendship is indeed as miraculous as a vaulted arch!

I would also like to take this opportunity to thank Series Editor Adam Sharr and Trudy Varcianna of Routledge for their friendly professionalism. I was able to complete this publication thanks to research leave granted by the research committee of my School of Fine Art, History of Art & Cultural Studies at the University of Leeds. I also acknowledge the benefit I have gained by being able to share my enthusiasm for Kant's cosmopolitical utopianism and architecture with our students.

Introduction

Why Kant now?

Up to now this series has presented key twentieth-century and contemporary 'thinkers for architects'. By contrast, this volume analyses the contribution that an eighteenth-century philosopher can make to thinking architectural theory and practice *now*. Despite Immanuel Kant's world being further away from us than that of more recent thinkers, we will see that his ideas nevertheless engage with issues that concern, or rather *should* concern, those involved with building today's and tomorrow's world.

In many ways architects carry a lot of responsibility for shaping and forming our present possibilities and future realisations. The quality of our environment is to some (undecidable) extent a determining factor for us, both as sentient and as intellectual beings. Architecture can stimulate our imagination and quicken our sense of being alive. It can also deaden our senses and limit our thoughts.

Back in the first century BC, Vitruvius had suggested that the ABC of architecture comprised: *firmitas* ('durability', 'solidity'), *utilitas* ('utility', 'convenience') and *venustas* ('beauty', 'grace'). He wrote that, for a building to last, its 'foundations have to be carried down to the solid ground and materials wisely and liberally selected' (Vitruvius 1960, 17). Its structural durability and the various ways it ages materially over time is a quality test for its *firmitas*. Its timespan might be limited, as in the case of temporary structures, but even for these there is no continuous present. The passage of time and the change it can bring about still have to be taken into account. For a building to have *utilitas*, 'the arrangement of the building [has to be] such that nothing hinders its use; each thing is assigned to its suitable and appropriate place'. Usefulness implies that a building should not be inappropriately or insufficiently 'designed' so that it fails to provide the spaces we need to carry out our various activities. It should probably also be borne in mind that too much supposed 'functionality' might also turn out to be 'dysfunctional' inasmuch as it leaves us nothing to make our own; everything has already been calculated and programmed for an all too abstract notion of the inhabitant. We cannot inhabit the spaces. Once again time, as temporality, is an issue: our needs can change, and we also have our own habits; a building, to be functional, has therefore to be adaptable and responsive. In short, for a building to have *venustas*, the 'form has to be agreeable and elegant thanks to the just proportions of all its parts' (Vitruvius 1960, 17; Cornu 2009, 15). Of course, tastes and conventions about what is harmonious and pleasing might also change over time. There might not be an eternal golden rule or even a consensus about what beauty is. Nevertheless, it is instructive for us to appreciate that, for Vitruvius, *venustas* – that is the ways a building pleases us aesthetically, the ways it appeals to us as potentially creative beings – was as important as *firmitas* and *utilitas*. For him, all three factors had to be present for architecture to take place. Following Vitruvius' lead, one may wonder just how much 'real' architecture actually takes place in our modern world with its many 'non-places' that propagate a capitalist 'global monoculture' (Augé 2008; Sachs 2010, 111ff.). Many of the ugly, corporatised spaces in which we spend substantial amounts of our time, while often also spending our money by eating, drinking and shopping, cannot be considered to be 'architectural' at all. Why do we put up with it? Given the centrality of the built environment in our lives, we should have higher expectations of what architecture is capable of materialising for us. We should place higher, 'aesthetic' demands on those whose capital literally shapes our world.

Even if Kant knew little about architecture as a practice, it is central to his philosophy. He refers to its solidity and utility as a way of defining what architecture is and describing his philosophical system. At first sight we might well find his conception of architecture to be restrictive, too rigid and lacking in imagination. For example, he might seem to have overlooked the important factor of temporality as outlined above. However, a closer look at his writings will reveal a much richer sense of what constructing in this evolving world involves. We will see that the issues facing us if we want to build effectively (i.e. according to the principle of *firmitas*) and purposively (i.e. complying with *utilitas*) are pertinently addressed by him. He was also an inspiring and challenging thinker of *venustas* (as well as the 'sublime', as we will see). For Kant, the appreciation of beauty 'quickens' the faculties of the imagination and understanding (Kant 1988a, §9). Through beauty we engage with a world and those beings within it in ways that are stimulating and capable of transforming the world in which we find ourselves. There is no way that for Kant corporatised 'design' could provide the aesthetically pleasing spaces that we need to be, not only as socialised individuals, but also as evolving beings who aspire to something different from the world we have now. A beautiful space is one wherein the 'free play of [our] powers of representation' can take place (Kant 1988a, §21). Beauty permits us to perceive alternatives to our contemporary situation. Just how many buildings fulfil Vitrivius' requirement for architecture to possess not only '*firmitas*' and '*utilitas*', but also '*venustas*' understood in these ways? Are not most of them compromises with the dominant world of global capitalism? Do they really meet our needs, not only those of the present, but also those of possible futures?

Thinkers presented in earlier volumes in this series have already asked themselves these same questions. To name just three of them: Walter Benjamin (see Elliott 2011), Martin Heidegger (see Sharr 2007) and Henri Lefebvre (see Coleman 2014b). In their different ways, these thinkers raised issues still pertinent for us now as critical thinkers of architecture. I will now briefly evoke some of Benjamin's, Heidegger's and Lefebvre's ideas, and then begin to indicate how Kant, from his eighteenth-century perspective, complements their twentieth-century views. By so staging such a *compossible* 'dialogue' between Kant and these more contemporary thinkers of architecture, we can learn a lot about the similarities and differences between Kant's world and 'ours'. I loosely use the philosopher Leibniz's term 'compossible' as a way of suggesting that the dialogue I envisage, while 'taking place' posthumously and retrospectively, *could still happen*. For Leibniz the world contains an infinite combination of possible things that could be brought into existence. The world is not closed-in on itself but is full of untapped potentiality waiting to be acted upon. Consequentially, temporality does not advance in a steadily linear fashion, mowing over what has been as something belonging to a dead and buried past, but instead consists of forked paths which offer us a variety of options whose outcomes are not always foreseeable (see, e.g. Leibniz 1969, 360–362; Deleuze 1985, 170–171). By implication I wish to suggest that Kant has much to say to us now, sometimes precisely because of his different situation. By actualising Kant's eighteenth-century ideas, we can enrich our historically informed sense of what architecture has been, is now, and *still could be*.

In 'The Work of Art in the Age of Its Technological Reproducibility' (1936), Walter Benjamin presented visual culture, especially film, as a revolutionary new medium. It had the potential to 'dynamite' the anachronistic forms, ranging from artworks to buildings, which for him defined the human environment. Until the arrival of the moving image, the human was artificially restrained within the inflexible and static 'prison world' of the modern city:

> Our bars and city streets, our offices and furnished rooms, our railroad stations and our factories, seemed to close relentlessly around us.
>
> (Benjamin 2002, 117, §xvi)

All too often our buildings are rooted in inadequate (whether anachronistic or inappropriately 'designed') conceptions of space that restrictively predetermine how we orientate ourselves. Emerging from these formalistic constraints, Benjamin detected radically new demands, particularly from 'the masses', for accommodation that better befits the dynamic world of modernity. Benjamin also identified actual places where richer, more vital and communal, forms of constructing the urban tissue were in play. For instance, a distinctive feature of the traditionally poorer districts of Naples, he suggested, was, and maybe still is, 'porosity' between the insides and the outsides of buildings (Benjamin 1996, 416). Indeed, such architectural fluidity stands in stark contrast to the carceral separation of an enclosed space from its outside, characteristic of many buildings today in this age of globalised capitalism, with its privatisation of public space. Benjamin also draws our attention to the utopian 'wish images' of the past (Benjamin 1999, 898). For example, Charles Fourier's communitarian project for a phalanstery – a co-operative community – held out the promise of still not-yet-fully explored potential for reconceiving how we might better live and work together (see Elliott 2011). In this book we will likewise see what Kant has to say about his eighteenth-century modernity. We will be considering to what extent his notion of architecture is permeable and flexible. We will see what he has to say about the limits that surround and determine us. We will also be looking at how his ideas might lead us to a more 'utopian' form of architecture, one that engages more with our possible futures, rather than accommodating itself to so-called present 'needs' and dominant 'market forces'.

In his essay 'Building, Dwelling, Thinking' – which was originally a speech given at a Darmstadt conference on the subject of 'Man and Space' in 1951 – Martin Heidegger talked about how the crisis-management of a housing shortage does not necessarily, indeed often does not, lead to an enriched sense of 'dwelling'. For Heidegger, many of the post Second World War housing schemes were just functional means to a short-term end. Despite serving the undeniably important purpose of providing immediate shelter, they nevertheless failed to address other fundamental needs relating to our destination as living, but finite, beings. Heidegger wrote:

> Today's houses may even be well planned, easy to keep, attractively cheap, open to air, light and sun, but – do the houses in themselves hold any guarantee that *dwelling* occurs in them?
>
> (Heidegger 1975, 146)

Citing the famous lines from Hölderlin's poem 'In lovely blueness/Full of merit, yet poetically, man/Dwells on this earth', Heidegger confronts us with the question: how can we build so as to 'dwell poetically' on this earth (Heidegger 1975, 213–229; Sharr 2007)? In his own way, Kant asks the same question as Heidegger. Despite seemingly tying architecture down to the very solidity and functionality that Heidegger is questioning as inadequate notions of the medium in which one dwells, we will see that Kant gives us a far wider and more inspiring vision of what architecture should be. Kant obliges us to ask ourselves the questions: who are we? Where are we heading? What should we do? His emphasis on constant critique as a form of resistance to any passive acceptance of how things supposedly 'are' is an important weapon to wield in any age of 'crisis'. It is important to hold onto the principle of one's autonomy, to one's hopes for a better future and not to succumb to normalising panic about the 'state of things'. Architects have rarely stood up to say 'no' to reactionary regimes. Philosophers also, Heidegger in Nazi Germany being a prime example, are far from having a glorious record for courageous, principled and imaginative counter-thinking and doing. Kant might have been an exception. At the very least,

<u>Kant's ideas and vision oblige us to think beyond a 'prefabricated' world into which we just have to fit. He requires us to make decisions and to be accountable for our actions.</u>

Henri Lefebvre was another thinker who was critical of the reduction of the built environment to series of preformatted 'products' which he read as a symptom of the debilitating and normalising repetition at large within society as a whole. This malady led him to ask the question: do these spaces still qualify as 'works' [*oeuvres*]? In *The Production of Space*, he wrote:

> It is obvious, sad to say, that repetition has everywhere defeated uniqueness, that the artificial and contrived have driven all spontaneity and naturalness from the field, and, in short, that products have vanquished works ... Can such a space still be called 'work' [*oeuvres*]?
>
> (Lefebvre 1991, 75)

For Lefebvre, the psychological outcomes of an environment which is monotonously repetitive are boredom and social disengagement, which in turn lead to a passive complicity with 'the order of the functional, bureaucratic city' (Lefebvre cited by Violeau 1999, 39). Whereas some early modernists, such as Benjamin, sometimes too optimistically considered quantity, the proliferation of mechanically reproducible copies, as sparking a 'qualitative transformation' of art forms that is progressive, mobilising and creative (Benjamin 2002, 107, §vi; Morgan 2008).

Lefebvre – 40 years on – sees its definite decline into a formatted, homogenising production of space and the bodies within it. Benjamin had welcomed visual culture for its democratising potential. He had also warned against its 'aestheticisation' of politics, detectable in the Nazis' use of modern technology whereby the whole of life under the totalitarian regime becomes one propagandistically organised 'work of art'. For Lefebvre, 'visualization' is killing 'culture'; it is becoming a way of thinking and doing that detrimentally affects the very walls we build to live in. Lefebvre clearly draws our attention to the dangerous effects that 'visualization' can have on the quality of our spaces in the following passage:

> a further important aspect of spaces of this kind is their increasingly pronounced visual character. They are made with the visible in mind: the visibility of people and things, of spaces and of whatever is contained by them. The predominance of visualization (more important than 'spectacularization', which is in any case subsumed by it), serves to conceal repetitiveness. People *look*, and take sight, take seeing, for life itself. We build on the basis of papers and plans. We buy on the basis of images. Sight and seeing, which in the Western tradition once epitomised intelligibility, have turned into a trap: the means whereby, in social space, diversity may be simulated and a travesty of enlightenment and intelligibility ensconced under the sign of transparency.
> (Lefebvre 1999, 75–76)

The motif of visibility and transparency evidently featured prominently in the discourse of the Enlightenment philosophy of the eighteenth century. Kant himself explains enlightenment as freeing ourselves from 'shadows', from superstitious beliefs that seek to condemn us to 'immaturity' (Kant 1994, 54–60). His philosophy aims to equip us with techniques for seeing the 'light'. Kant's world undeniably predated our age of omnipresent visual culture with its highly sophisticated, mobile technologies. Nevertheless, technology and the global communication it facilitated did play a constitutive role in his writings (see Morgan 2007, 35–46). He also addressed the issues of mediatisation, instrumentalisation and consumer 'culture' evoked by Lefebvre. We will consider the similarities and differences between Kant's world and ours in the light of these topics.

For these three recent thinkers – Benjamin, Heidegger, Lefebvre – architecture, the art of building, is embroiled with social concerns. Architecture can contribute either positively or negatively to the construction of our world. Those practising architecture should feel responsible for how they build, with what means and to what ends. Immanuel Kant also obliges us to confront these issues. His work was informed by a concern for the world as an evolving whole and how our acts, as particular instances of decision-making, have repercussions within a wider framework. According to Kant, in an interconnected and dynamic world, humans should act as mutually dependent and responsible subjects; they should behave 'cosmopolitically', i.e. orienting themselves in relation to the planet as a whole.

Given his future-oriented and ethico-politically concerned thinking, Kant is a thinker who clearly should speak to architects.

Those engaged in creative construction are necessarily trained in negotiating between theory and practice. As such they are ideal readers of Kant, as his critical project precisely consisted of testing and exploring the viability of ideas, so as to ascertain to what extent and, crucially, *how* ideas could have a positive bearing on the whole world and on us as active agents therein. However, Kant has been generally ill-served by secondary criticism: the image one generally has of him is that of a thinker whose works are inaccessible and therefore off-putting. The aim of this volume to the series is to demonstrate how his ideas bear pertinently and creatively upon the world in which we live *now* and for which we should care thoughtfully. However, by so doing the intention is not just to demonstrate the interest of Immanuel Kant's architecturally related ideas simply in and on their own terms. I also wish to use Kant's writings as an opportunity to evoke certain issues that strike me as being particularly relevant for architects, or indeed for everyone interested in the built environment. Regardless of whether we are professional architects or not, it is surely in all of our interests to invest in the spatial quality, in the aesthetic, political, social, ecological composition, of our surroundings? Even if we are not consciously aware of it, architecture impinges on all of us in ways that other 'art forms' do not necessarily. Hence Benjamin suggested that we absorb the architectural work of art collectively in a distracted way, not necessarily with the eye of a concentrated specialist (Benjamin 2002, 120, §xviii). Accordingly, the aim of the 'Thinkers for Architects' series is maybe not so much to present the case each time for the 'necessity' for those interested in architecture to acquire, in any sense, an 'expert' knowledge of a particular thinker's ideas, as if they possessed value in and of themselves. The objective is perhaps more to build up a constellation of different viewpoints through which various architectural issues are refracted.

Hence, while greatly appreciating Colin Davies' interesting book, *Thinking About Architecture*, and taking on board his emphasis on the greater importance of a 'thematic approach' to architectural theory compared to a more precious commitment to a particular thinker's world view, the criticism made of this series maybe suggests a greater divide between his concerns and ours than is actually the case. It is doubtless not the intention of this series that architects become philosophers (Davies 2011, 8). It is however also not the assumption of this series that 'curiosity' for architecture is limited to those professionally engaged in the profession (Davies 2011, 9). It is therefore hoped that, for example, *Kant for Architects* will appeal to a wider public. Everyone has an opinion about what is loosely called 'architecture'; we live with it, though we often just put up with it.

<u>We need to actively reinvest in architecture as a polemical field of theory and practice so as to realise our vested interests in building an environment that provides a groundwork for a more positive future world.</u>

Paradoxically we can sometimes gain a sense of what might be possible for the future by looking into what we deem to be the past. Looking backwards, for example, at Kant's world and ideas, can make visible to us what is no longer current or pertinent, as well as revealing a different, 'utopian' perspective that could suggest to us otherwise unseen potentialities for the future. The layout for this book is as follows:

Chapter 1 situates Kant in relation to his now largely destroyed birthplace and life-long home, Königsberg. We will examine how his specific city featured in his writings on cosmopolitics (i.e. thinking and feeling as part of the whole earth, beyond boundaries). We will examine his ideas about place, experience, knowledge and moral responsibility. By alluding to the chequered history of Königsberg, we will then ask questions about our relationship to such obscured places, and what sort of future could be built for them in the future.

Chapter 2 continues this reflection on the wider implications of our thinking and doing by examining Kant's notion of 'critique'. This analysis necessitates an examination of Kant's metaphorical use of architecture and its underlying assumptions, notably about what architecture is basically about and what homely dwelling consists of. Widening our understanding of what constitutes 'good' construction is an important aspect of this book.

Chapter 3 will examine how the criterion of beauty in Kant's *Critique of Judgement* interferes with a notion of 'the good'. Kant's analysis presents not only us, but also himself, with a series of challenges to any attempt to categorise architecture definitively either as a 'proper' Fine Art, or as a subsidiary art form principally concerned with functionality. We will explore his ideas by means of a specific contemporary example (Frank Gehry's La Fondation Louis Vuitton), in order to raise issues about architecture's relation to commodity culture.

Chapter 4 continues this analysis of aesthetic judgement. We consider the role architecture, nature and technology play in Kant's presentation of the sublime. We will critique a version of the sublime in relation to contemporary concerns about ecology and sustainable development. The chapter will then revisit Kant's critical project. It suggests how more alternative forms of architecture – the specific example is Buckminster Fuller's tensegrity structures – could yield us a vision of what forms Kant's 'sublime' cosmopolitical future might take. The intention is to remind ourselves that this world is far from being completely prefabricated, and that it is incumbent upon ourselves creatively to cultivate a sense of our potential for individual and collective agency. It was what Kant hoped for us.

CHAPTER 1

Placing Kant

The city of Königsberg/Kaliningrad

Notoriously, Kant's constitutional walks through the city of Königsberg were so regular, and therefore predictable, that his fellow citizens did not need watches to know the time of day. Indeed, the poet and essayist Heinrich Heine rather mockingly wrote:

> The history of Kant's life is difficult to describe. For he neither had a life nor a history. He lived a mechanically ordered, almost abstract, bachelor life in a quiet out-of-the-way lane in Königsberg, an old city at the northeast border of Germany. I do not believe that the large clock of the Cathedral there completed its task with less passion and less regularity than its fellow citizen Immanuel Kant. Getting up, drinking coffee, writing, giving lectures, eating, taking a walk, everything had its set time, and the neighbours knew precisely it was 3.30 pm when Kant stepped outside his door with his gray coat and Spanish stick in his hand.
>
> (Heine, cited in in Kühn 2001, 14)

This description of Kant certainly gives us the impression that he was neither what might be called a Benjaminian *flâneur* engaged in apparently idle perambulations around the city that have been interpreted as actually constituting a 'demonstration against the division of labour', nor a Lefebvrian mobile 'rhythmanalyst' whose attentiveness to his own body and its surrounding environment as composed of varying 'bundles, bouquets, garlands of rhythms' has also been read as resisting the reification brought about by commodity capitalism (Benjamin 2002 427, M5,8; Lefebvre 2004, 3, 20). If Kant's experiences of spatiality were really so controlled and restricted, he was indeed not someone who was interested in intrepidly exploring the interstices of the urban fabric. He was no metropolitan explorer who openly embraced chance encounters in the name of resisting dominant trends of being that format our responses to the world in which we live.

To be sure, Kant's limited experience of urbanity in the East Prussian city of Königsberg did not expose him to many characteristics of our highly charged metropolitan lives. He was neither confronted with the same scale of urban development nor probably with the same complexity of lifestyle. Nevertheless, we will see that Kant had a keener sense of the importance and potentiality of space and the human individual's particular place within it than he is usually given credit for. His philosophy cannot be detached from a consideration of our human 'situatedness' on this spherical planet. While encouraging us to become citizens of the world, he emphasised that this cosmopolitical engagement necessitates us also being responsible actants in our local here and now (Kant 1994, 51). His writing bears in mind not only a global context but also how we have to, in an ongoing fashion, orientate ourselves within our immediate vicinity, finding our way each time, even during the most habitual of our walks (Kant 1994, 238–239). Hence, his own personal context featured prominently in his writings. For example, in his *Anthropology from a Pragmatic Point of View* he wrote:

> A city such as Königsberg on the river Pregel – a large city, the centre of a state, the seat of the government's provincial councils, the site of a university (for cultivation of the sciences), a seaport connected by rivers with the interior of the country, so that its location favours traffic with the rest of the country as well as with neighbouring or remote countries having different languages and customs – is a suitable place for broadening one's knowledge of man and the world. In such a city, this knowledge can be acquired even without travelling.
>
> (Kant 1974a, 4)

In the past, Königsberg was known as 'the Venice of the North' because of its many bridges across the river Pregel. Kant highlighted the importance of this river. The Pregel, which is fed by tributaries, used to ferry traders and their goods from many towns, cities and villages situated both within and outside Prussian territorial boundaries. This fluid thoroughfare not only provided a prime means by which commercial exchanges took place throughout the kingdom, but also provided the channel through which goods were further transported to other parts of the globe. Kant deemed that such a place – at once rich in local specificity yet substantially populated and transited by well-travelled foreigners – served as a fertile context for the accumulation of knowledge of the world as a whole. The port city provided a particularly fruitful articulation between the local and the global, and between different modes of existence – the terrestrial and the maritime. It combined the mapped-outness of the human appropriation of land together with the recalcitrant inhospitality of the ocean, which, however many territorial rights are applied to the sea, remains challengingly alien to us.

Kant considered that the rich textuality of space, the multifarious interfaces, that the port city provided was a good environment for fostering a pluralistic frame of mind. Again in *Anthropology*, he wrote:

> The opposite of egoism can only be *pluralism*, that is, the attitude of not being occupied with oneself as the whole world, but regarding and conducting oneself as a citizen of the world.
>
> (Kant 1974a, 12)

Crucial to this recognition of the world as existing outside of ourselves – of relocating ourselves as one person among others (as one part of a whole), who has the right to be respected but who in turn should take into account the perspectives of those around him – is place.

Kant stresses that, in order to have an informed sense of humans as an evolving species, we need to synthesise an in-depth immersion in our local, regional and national culture

with an expanded awareness – via travel or, a good alternative according to him, through travel writing – of foreign customs and ways of life.

He wrote: 'One of the ways of extending the range of anthropology is travelling, or at least reading travelogues' (Kant 1974a, 4). Kant's anthropological writings are interested in investigating what the human 'as a free agent makes, or can and should make, of himself', i.e. with the possible journeys he could undergo (Kant 1974a, 3). Rather than analysing the human as predetermined by the 'play of nature', Kant's 'pragmatic' anthropology invests in the human as an active citizen of, and in, a cosmopolitical world yet to come (Foucault 2008, 33 44, 54–55). A more creative sense of his potential to contribute to worldly relations can be garnered through an exposure to alterity. An exposure to cultural difference can provoke one to entertain alternative ways of being; it can foster an extended space of psychical generosity. Kant suggests that certain sorts of physical places particularly favour this type of cultural and moral education. He advocates that his particular location, in the busy port – and university – city of Königsberg, where he spent all of his long life (he died at the age of 80), was such a place. It provided a fertile context, a hospitable site, for anthropological enquiry, cosmopolitan exchange and cosmopolitical development.

We might well think that Kant overstates his case by assuming that everybody who lives in a place like Königsberg is *de facto* a liberal-minded cosmopolitan or citizen of the world. I will consider two main objections to his analysis so as to draw attention to important issues relating to architecture.

First, we might object to his portrayal of Königsberg as a city, considering it to be politically naïve, not to say negligent of historical truths. However open-mindedly multicultural the Hanseatic city of Königsberg was, with its conversational meeting places (its coffee houses and salons) and its prestigious university, the Albertina (founded in 1544) with its significant Polish and Lithuanian student population, such busy mercantile centres built their financial and cultural wealth on the back of overseas colonies and local serfdom, and indeed often continue to do so. Lisbet Koerner (see below my remarks about the conditions of subcontracted building site workers) gives us some insight into the socio-economic reality of the Baltic region during the Enlightenment period when she writes:

> In Baltic Russia and Sweden, the German nobility, incorporated in the knightly orders of Livonia, Estonia, Lithuania, East Prussia, Courland and Oesel, exploited their Lithuanian, Estonian and Latvian serfs with impunity ... There was little local opposition to these slave regimes. The South and East Baltic shores were dotted with diaspora trading cities whose German patriciates carefully guarded their independence (an independence inherited from the Hanseatic League but eroded throughout the century, especially in Prussia). Neither they nor the German nobles particularly worried themselves about the subjugated native peoples of the East Baltic, peoples they still – after five hundred years – conceptualised only vaguely, as *Sklaven* (slaves), *Undeutsche* (non-Germans) or *Graue* (gray ones).
>
> (Koerner 1999, 404–405)

Regrettably, Kant does not nuance his eulogy of Königsberg in the *Anthropology* by making an explicit link between his impressive and influential city and its extensive exploited hinterland. However, it should be noted that elsewhere he did deplore the 'cruellest and most calculated' slavery which he knew existed in the Sugar Islands (Kant 1994 107–108). He also wrote a postscript lending his support to the Prussian Christian Gottlieb Mielcke's promotion of Lithuanian culture in the guise of a Lithuanian–German dictionary. In this text Kant underscores the importance of fostering the 'particular characteristics' of this 'ancient people'. By so doing, J. D. Mininger suggests, Kant was: 'putting his name on the line, for a political cause, for Lithuanians, and for the project of Enlightenment within the entire eastern Prussian and Baltic region' (Mininger and Kant 2005, 12). He thereby showed that he was not completely blind to the social injustices and abuses of power which give the lie to the spectacular impressions cities make on us. Posing the question about the cost – who paid or pays it in hard labour, in suffering and sometimes in death? – for metropolitan splendour is no minor issue. We only have to think of today's mega-cities with their monumental constructions, and the fate of the vulnerable migrant workers who often build them, to understand the far-reaching social effects architecture can have. Such reflection can then lead us on to consider the political responsibilities of architects towards not only their clients, the users of their buildings and the environment, but also towards those involved in the construction process itself, however 'subcontracted' they might be. To be rigorous, any portrayal of a historic city, especially one like Kant's that uses it as a model for a thinking and doing 'cosmopolitically', in the name of 'humanity as a whole', should pay attention to the exploited voices enmeshed in its fine urban fabric.

Second, we might be left unconvinced by Kant's enthusiastic espousal of travel, whether it takes the form of actual delocalisation to or, alternatively, reading travel literature about foreign places, as a means of broadening one's mind about the human species. There is no guarantee that the mentality produced by going to see others, let alone just reading about them from the comfort of one's urban armchair, is 'cosmopolitan' in the sense of making us embrace an expansive idea of humanity 'as a whole' towards whom one should act responsibly. Just because, in one's 'multicultural' environment, one is exposed to the varying ways of life and perhaps economic plights of others, one might nevertheless not feel oneself at all obliged to behave ethically towards them. Indeed, the opposite might well be the case. One might return from one's physical or virtual voyages, or even from more local perambulations in different ethnic neighbourhoods, more perplexed than intrigued by other ways of constructing and experiencing the world. One might even return home more convinced than before of one's own cultural 'superiority'.

Hence, Kant's, on one level, idealised portrayal of Königsberg as a place that nurtures an especially rich relation to the rest of the world for its (privileged) inhabitants provokes us to address many probing topics. Architects have often deliberated about the extent our mentality and cultural outlook is related, or even determined, by place, by the specific sites they project into this world. As thinkers of architecture presumably interested in fostering multiculturalism, we should ask ourselves how far it can be furthered by particular types of spaces. What sorts of public and private spheres do and could we inhabit and what encounters with alterity do they facilitate or pre-empt? These were questions of great importance for Kant (see, e.g. Kant 1994, 54–60). Do compact cities, such as the former Königsberg, positively encourage multiculturalism? Maybe they do. Can well-designed, integrated architecture provide propitious conditions for a better and more enlightened world? Maybe it can. Probably poor design does not positively encourage psychological openness and generosity. To be culturally creative in a sprawling non-place often requires energetic resistance and a militant reclaiming and determined reinscription of space. Be that as it may, can Kant, he who never left Königsberg, really claim that his birth – and death – place was a 'fitting place' for 'broadening [his] knowledge of man and the world' (Kant 1974a, 4; 1977, 400)?

Even if intrepid travellers can turn out to be prejudiced bigots who transport their ways of behaving with them, actually physically exposing oneself to foreign places, to different climates, to strangers with their curious customs, often shakes up one's cultural assumptions. Kant, however, makes claims for the comparable benefits of armchair tourism by means of travel literature. This advocacy encourages us to ask further pertinent questions concerning our contemporary notions of place and our relation to technology. For example, is today's virtual travel via global communication networks equivalent to the vicarious 'experiences' and/or 'knowledge' on offer – if they indeed are – with traditional, book-based literature about 'foreign parts'? Of course the very nature of distant lands is itself constantly being changed by these same global communications (by relatively low-cost travel, publicity, widely available 'information', e.g. in the form of blogs). The histories of foreign destinations are also packaged with the tourist economy in mind. We are maybe increasingly being sold exotic 'authenticity' before we even arrive in a place, as well as throughout our stay there. How do these considerations impact on architecture which might be concerned with conserving, or at least dialoguing with, some notion of the 'vernacular', with what is 'local' and/or 'indigenous'?

How do global technologies impact on our conception and experience of public and private space, and on our appreciation of specific places?

However important Königsberg was as an international meeting place back in the eighteenth century, Kant is probably not justified in thinking that, by right of being one of its citizens, he is thus suitably qualified to pronounce on the composition of our planet, its various peoples, their ways and their environment, as he does, notably in his lectures on *Physical Geography*. Such an ungrounded stance can easily be castigated for the racist stereotyping it produces, or taken as a sign of ignorant times, or dismissed as preposterous (see Eze 1997, 58–64). As we already saw in the Heine passage above, Kant as a person has also been a butt of jokes. Despite being influential during his lifetime and still acknowledged as one of the most important philosophers today, he is now rarely considered fashionable, let alone 'sexy'. Critics have often unashamedly permitted themselves the licence to pass damning judgement on his ostensibly mundane personal life and the provincial mentality they consider it to have produced. For instance, in 'Youth Restored' (1933) the Russian writer Mikhail Zoshcenko (1894–1958) judged that Kant's life 'cannot be considered to be ideal insofar as he who leads it is in fact a mere machine' (cited by Goulga 1985 175–176). The philosopher Friedrich Nietzsche, whose own intense and ultimately tragic life continues to fascinate us, claimed that Kant was a 'fanatic of the Thou shalt', that he was always moralistically bossing us around (Nietzsche 1968, 474, §888). He deduces that Kant was not a 'real human being' (Nietzsche 1987 181; 1990, 134).

Despite the bad odds, Kant's recent biographer, Manfred Kühn, reckons that, despite his having spent all of his time on this planet in Königsberg, Kant did nevertheless 'have a life', indeed quite a sociable one at that (Kühn 2001, 20). Kühn also makes it clear that he wants to steer his analysis of the socio-historical situation of eighteenth-century Königsberg midway between that of critics who present the town as a dull and stagnant 'backwater', and Kant's own idealisation of the town as a 'fit place for acquiring ... knowledge of the world' (Kühn 2001,

55–60). So, given these various options, how are we going to position ourselves in relation to the city of Königsberg? This question demands a response. I am going to argue that, as thinkers of architecture, we should have something to say about such places. Even we, who might not have even visited 'Königsberg', should be deemed in some way 'responsible' towards such places. Indeed, Kant himself might well suggest that such an involvement is precisely what is implied in being 'cosmopolitical' citizens on this planet. In other words, Kant's 'cosmopolitics' obliges us to engage responsibly with such places, however far removed from us we might feel they are. What would such an engagement involve?

Königsberg's history tells us much about the varied lives cities and their inhabitants can have. It can also challenge us to think about what might be needed to put such places 'back on the map'. Today's 'Kaliningrad' (it was renamed in 1945 when it became Soviet territory) is both a city and an oblast of the Russian Federation, despite being sandwiched between the two European Union member states of Poland and Lithuania, and situated 300 km from the Russian border. This curious exclave has had an interesting and chequered past, and maybe still has a future. It was founded by Teutonic knights in the thirteenth century. It was the capital city of East Prussia from 1772 to 1829 and 1878 to 1945, and of the Province of Prussia from 1829 to 1878. It was largely destroyed during and in the aftermath of the Second World War. When the Soviets arrived, its German population was forcibly expelled. For some historians this event was an instance of 'terrible revenge' or even of 'ethnic cleansing' (de Zayas 1994). This issue remains highly sensitive and controversial. During the Soviet period, Kaliningrad was a mysterious military zone of strategic importance because of the port of Baltiisk, situated just outside the city of Königsberg. Baltiisk was the only port in Russia to be ice-free all year round. In recent years Kaliningrad has far less geopolitical importance (even if, were we to fall back into another Cold War, it might always re-emerge as a contested territorial issue). If the film *Three Days* (1991), made by the Lithuanian director Sharunas Bartas, is anything to go by, the city is lost, suspended in a strange, disquieting state of exception. The following description has been given of this film:

Bartas' characters well fit the dismal, depressing footage of Kaliningrad. None of the five characters reveal much about themselves. It is clear however that deep emotions are hidden behind the silent faces. It is the day in day out misery and hopelessness that depresses them and ruins their communication. Bartas uses subtle means and images, behind which an enormous tension broods. A young generation is forcefully suppressed by hopelessness.

(www.moskwood.nl, accessed 16 September 2014)

What might the future hold for a place like Kaliningrad given that its present situation sounds so bleak? The current predicament of the city and of the whole area is at once specific to its particular, traumatic history, and one that port cities generally have had to face in these so-called 'post-industrial' times. Indeed, economic shifts and new technology have meant that the integrated port city, a long-standing feature of urban history, has become anachronistic. In *European Port-Cities in Transition*, Hoyle and Pinder analyse the crucial role port cities have played throughout centuries of urban history. They write:

> The cityport, or port-city, is one of the quintessential elements of the European space economy, symbolizing the fusion of cultural diversity and historical experience that characterize this focal world politico-economic region. A close association between cities and ports is a recurrent theme throughout the history of European civilization. From the ancient Mediterranean cultures to the present era of international cooperation and development, 'cities appear as a constant in every civilization' (Konvitz, 1978, xi) and ports serve as transport modes facilitating economic growth at different scales. In temporal and spatial terms, therefore, European port cities and the regions they serve constitute a fundamental element in the spatial organization and reorganization of economies and societies, and in the relations between those societies and the environment within which they are set.
>
> (Hoyle and Pinder 1992, 2)

Hoyle and Pinder further explain that this coexistence and interactive growth of the port and its city generally continued from medieval times up to the late nineteenth century/early twentieth century, when rapid commercial and industrial expansion forced ports to start developing beyond the city confines for the first time. The mid-twentieth century saw further industrial growth, a particularly significant factor in which was the development of roll-on–roll-off facilities. The disassociation of the port from the city and the retreat from its waterfront was further aggravated between the 1960s and 1980s as changes in maritime technology – bigger vessels and the subsequent need for deeper waters – induced the growth of separate maritime industrial developmental areas. The situation has recently become even more aggravated with the invention of Triple E ships. These gigantic container vessels have a length equivalent to 43 London buses or four jets lined up end-to-end. They can transport 18,000 20-foot containers (enough to fill a train 68 miles long, e.g. 180 million Apple iPods or 111 million pairs of trainers). As a consequence of these technological developments (that have arisen out of shifts in global manufacturing and consumer markets), many extra-city ports are in turn no longer able to adapt sufficiently to receive them.

A recent feature of many 'post-industrial' port cities has been the redevelopment of their abandoned waterfronts in the search for a new lease of life for the very zones that were once the hub of metropolitan activity and economic prosperity (e.g. Nantes, Lyon, Liverpool). Such a metamorphosis was famously, some would say notoriously, achieved in Bilbao apparently thanks to Frank Gehry's Guggenheim museum (1997). By most accounts his conspicuous stamp produced such special effects that the whole city was subsequently galvanised into renewed action. Apparently architects can really make the earth move when they want to!

Places like Kaliningrad, however important in the past, however intriguing as a contemporary geopolitical conundrum (should it be 'returned' to Germany? Should it be tied closer to the Russian Federation? Should it become an independent state, e.g. within the European Union or become part of Poland or Lithuania?), however desperate a place to live in now, probably cannot hope for the same make-over treatment as Bilbao. A 'starchitect' like Gehry is not likely to build there. How could such a project possibly be financed? Who would be interested in investing in such a place?

There is more to architecture than landmark monuments – so spectacular, so 'rich' – designed by signature architects.

Indeed, as Bernard Rudofsky so evocatively documented in *Architecture without Architects* – I will be returning to him shortly – modest 'anonymous builders' can also build structures of great ingenuity and beauty. And, in any case, even if Kaliningrad cannot produce the examples of 'nonpedigreed architecture' that Rudofsky has in mind, it might be considered appropriate that those who are interested in urban history and cultural memory and engaged with social issues should always feel responsible for all such places in need of regeneration. Kant's Königsberg, even if it can no longer entertain us, as it did the mathematician Leonhard Euler (1707–1783), with its famous seven bridges across the Pregel, is certainly one such place.

As we have seen in this chapter, Kant made great claims for the cosmopolitical specificity of his homeplace. The port city of Königsberg was presented as a 'suitable place for broadening one's knowledge of man and the world' (Kant 1974a, 4). Today's Kaliningrad, which might be thought to be a non-place that probably features little in most people's cartographical imaginaries, cannot fulfil the same function that it did for Kant. Nevertheless, his conception of the human as both locally situated and as an active citizen of the world provoked us to interrogate our relation to such sites, and to consider how global technologies have transformed our relation to place. As we will see in the next chapter, questioning how we orientate ourselves and what we tend to take for granted, is in the spirit of Kantian critique.

CHAPTER 2

Kant, the critical project and architecture

While Immanuel Kant's philosophical writings have the reputation of being dauntingly difficult and opaque, he expressly wanted his philosophy to be popular, recognising that positive social change was incumbent on turning theory into general practice as much as possible. For him the challenge to thinking was that:

> The aim of every step in cultural progress which is man's education is to assign this knowledge and skill he has acquired to the world's use.
>
> (Kant 1974, 3)

In order to do so, we have to get a sense of what we can know, what questions are worth asking and which ones ultimately run the risk of dissipating our energy and wasting our time. As he writes in *Critique of Pure Reason:*

> Human reason has this peculiar fate that in some species of its knowledge it is burdened by questions which, as prescribed by the very nature of reason itself, it is not able to ignore, but which as transcending all its powers, it is not able to answer.
>
> (Kant 1983, Avii)

Our desire for knowledge is often insatiable. This drive is not necessarily a bad one. We should definitely 'dare to know' for ourselves; indeed, it is a condition for our personal and general 'enlightenment'. We certainly shouldn't renege on our responsibility towards ourselves, and ultimately towards others, by just passively accepting what others – the state, parents, teachers, priests – tell us about how things supposedly 'are'. Indeed, Kant's notion of critique and his keen sense of the world as *evolving* necessitates a spirited rejection of the very notion of a status quo, i.e. of an existing state of affairs that is to be maintained and upheld often passively and unquestioningly.

Accordingly, in 'On the Common Saying: "This May be True in Theory but it does not Apply in Practice" ', Kant rebukes cynics who refuse to entertain alternatives to the supposed status quo because of lack of empirical proof that things can be changed. Kant states that often projects 'which are founded only on hope' are rejected out of hand just because they do not as yet exist in the world (Kant 1994, 89). He points out that this fatalistic doom would have precluded such marvellous inventions as 'aerostatic balloons' (Kant 1994, 89). Balloons permit us to see the earth from above, thereby at least temporarily releasing us from our landlubberish flatness and encouraging us to adopt a different perspective on our planet. The proliferation of such different viewpoints of our globe can generate for us a better, more generous and open, sense of the world as a complex and dynamic whole (Morgan 2013, 120–139; see also Chapter 4). Of course, the same technology, ballooning, can also be instrumentalised by the military, as a means of reconnaissance and for ballistic purposes. Any technology is evidently not intrinsically 'good'; its 'nature' depends on the ethical end it is put to serve. Often good intentions find themselves being co-opted by destructive and retrograde political forces that nefariously undermine the 'utopian' vision of a 'perpetual peace' that Kant holds out to us in his 1795/6 essay. The key passage from this seminal essay, to which we will have occasion to return in Chapter 4, reads as follows:

> The peoples of the earth have thus entered in varying degrees into a universal community, and it has developed to the point where a violation of rights in *one* part of the world is felt *everywhere*. The idea of a cosmopolitan right is therefore not fantastic and exaggerated: it is a necessary extension to the unwritten code of political and international right, for public human rights generally, as thus for perpetual peace. Only under this condition can we flatter ourselves that we are continually advancing towards a perpetual peace.
>
> (Kant 1994, 107–108 [translation slightly modified]).

The 'feeling' evoked by Kant of being affected by the violation of human rights in another part of the world is increasingly facilitated by global networks of communication. Of course in today's technologised world it is even easier for us, as 'peoples of the [same] earth', to tune into the shockwaves that atrocities provoke. However, as we are well aware, the rapid facility with which we can access this information can in itself be problematic: overexposure, especially to images, can engender compassion fatigue and even blasé indifference. Thomas Hirschhorn's video 'Touching Reality' (2012) provides a graphic illustration of such an attitude: we see fingers scrolling through an amalgam of mangled bodies on the web. Sporadically an image of a corpse is prised open so as to peer at it more closely, maybe voyeuristically; we are uncomfortably unsure of the motivation behind the 'search'. In any case, the enlarged victim – whether limbless, decapitated or not, it ultimately does not seem really to matter – remains contextless, unidentified, without a history. The apparently nonchalant gesture of scrolling then resumes. Hirschhorn's video thereby forcefully throws into doubt our easy presumption that we are more informed about, and concerned by, what is going on in the real world nowadays just because it appears on our screens at the touch of our finger tips.

All the more reason, Kant would argue, to be vigilant, to ask questions, to feel implicated. Since there is the possibility of a global cosmopolitical 'public sphere' to which we can to 'varying degrees' have access, we *should* feel interpellated by such testimonies of violence. Despite the possible risk of failure, it is necessarily incumbent upon us to struggle for justice and a better world even while being bound by contractual obligations as, for example, teachers or practising architects, in our narrower 'private' sphere of activity (Kant 1994, 55). We are accountable for the binding nature of our compromises even if, or rather, especially as, there is no biblical Day of Judgement.

Kant is at once inspiring and highly demanding. He spurs us all on actively to further possibilities for positive change sometime in the future.

He refuses short-sighted objections which aim to ground 'utopian' projects, such as 'perpetual peace' (as well as ballooning) before they are given a chance to take off. Such faint-hearted excuses do not carry any weight for him. Their irrelevance is especially evident when it comes to moral aims 'which, so long as it is not demonstrably impossible to fulfil them, amount to duties' (Kant, 1994, 89). Kant laments what he sees as the 'sententious, inactive times' in which he lived (Kant, 1994, 63). There is far too much hot air and not enough action in this world. By demonstrating that theory can be put into practice, that we 'should assume' that what 'ought to be' is 'possible (in praxis)', Kant wants to reenergise his contemporaries' sense of agency so that the ills of fatalism, apathy, complicity with the dominant ideology, could eventually be overcome (Kant, 1994, 63, 92; Morgan 2014, 126–130). Recently it was fashionable to describe our age as 'postmodern'. We were characterised as being suspicious of Enlightenment's 'grand narratives' announcing 'progress'. We were allegedly cynical about the possibility of radical change and even sceptical about its desirability. Is this still the case? Maybe now we can appreciate the energetic potentiality in Kant's stance, which offers us a form of resistance to defeatism, which spurs us to refuse accepting the world 'as it is', dominated by the injustices of global capitalism.

Kant wrote of his century: '[Our] epoch is in especial degree, the epoch of critique, and to critique everything must submit.' For him not only religion and law-giving, but also reason itself had to be subjected to critique: 'The matured judgement of the epoch issues a call to reason to undertake anew the most difficult of all its tasks, that of self-knowledge' (Kant 1983, Axi 9). For him a lot is at stake: the very possibility of peace sometime in the future, instead of the recurrent destruction of warfare, hinges on critical thinking. If reason does not scrutinise not only the things (including ideas) around us, but also itself, it is in a 'state of nature, and can establish and secure its assertions and claims only through war', he asserts (Kant 1983, B779). For him these are critical times. Maybe the finite time we have to live on this planet should *always* be considered to be *especially* critical.

Kant makes it clear that if we squander opportunities for change and resign ourselves to 'presentism', to a notion of an ineluctable present, we fall short of our potentiality as a species. He tells us that:

> a universal cosmopolitan existence [is] the matrix within which all the original capacities of the human race are developed.
>
> (Kant 1994, 51)

Hence we certainly should not lapse into a depressive apathy about this world, its past and its future.

It is incumbent upon us to invest in Life, viewed as an ongoing series of processes informed by different points of view

(Morgan and Banham 2007, 35–46; 2013, 120–122). This is an important aspect of what is meant by 'cosmopolitics'. We will see that this idea has far-reaching architectural implications.

In the meantime, while we are preparing ourselves to embrace 'multiperspectivity', Kant warns us that we should recognise that neither everything, nor everyone, including ourselves, is always interesting. To think intensely and effectively, and not to be distracted, or even driven mad, by unbridled speculation about unimportant and nonsensical issues requires a robust sense of orientation. However, one should also be very wary of being dogmatic, of assuming that one is right. Equally, one should not take anything for granted just because we are told to. Kant asks a lot when he requires us to negotiate these competing demands on our powers of reason. We are told to discipline our reason ourselves, to auto-subject it to critique:

> Reason must in all its undertaking subject itself to criticism; should it limit freedom of criticism by any prohibitions, it must harm itself, drawing upon itself a damaging suspicion. *Nothing is so important through its usefulness,*

nothing so sacred, that it may be exempted from this searching examination, which knows no respect for persons. Reason depends on this freedom for its very existence. For reason has no dictatorial authority; its verdict is always simply the agreement of free citizens, of whom each one must be permitted to express, without let or hindrance, his objections or even his veto.

(Kant 1983, B766; *my italics*)

Critique is, at least for the time being, an ongoing questioning of our lives while conferring upon others the dignified status of 'free citizens'; that is to say while considering them capable of being autonomous thinkers with viewpoints that we should take into consideration. However, it is imperative that those who try to enforce their opinions in an authoritarian way be resisted. Kant's analysis thus draws our attention to competing pressures on our reasoning faculty: the ones that originate from outside, that we should sometimes incorporate, sometimes resist; and the ones that stem from within ourselves that can either productively drive us to extend our minds beyond the range of our possible experience, or that can drive us 'off-course', thereby dissipating our energy in futile speculation about questions that cannot be settled definitively. In other words, it might in the end be neither particularly helpful, nor ultimately stimulating to pronounce dogmatically on cosmological questions concerning the 'sum total of appearances in the world' (Kant 1983, B391). Presuming to know 'the supreme cause of the world' is maybe a less interesting standpoint to maintain than affirmatively working with a qualitative and productive difference between what is intelligible (i.e. a thing in itself that 'can never, indeed, be immediately known', that is not an object of possible experience (Kant 1983, B568) and what belongs to the sensible world of appearances. Indeed the ways these two realms can be co-ordinated is a constant challenge facing humans as 'rational beings' who are not completely in control. However, working with these contours can be more vitalising than indulging in the formless 'slumber of fictitious conviction'. Fully licensed 'extravagance' that leads to error is neither particularly interesting nor helpful (Kant 1983, B739). Our time on this planet is finite: one surely does not want to waste it unnecessarily?

Kant is complex and unrelenting. In 'Answer to the Question: What is Enlightenment?', he tells us that we should 'dare to know' about our world and not take things for granted; indeed he even holds us gravely responsible for our own lack of autonomy:

> A man may for his own person, and even then only for a limited period, postpone enlightening himself in matters he ought to know about. But to renounce such enlightenment completely, whether for his own person or even more so for generations, means violating and trampling underfoot the sacred rights of mankind.
>
> (Kant 1994, 58)

However, he does draw the distinction between our limits [*Grenzen*] and our limitations [*Schranken*]. J. W. Goethe, the poet, dramatist, novelist, scientist – what was he not? – had an interesting understanding of the value of Kant's philosophy for understanding natural process and artworks. He provides us with a means to explore this distinction between limits [*Grenzen*] and limitations [*Schranken*]. About the former he wrote:

> The slightest person can be complete if he moves within the limits [*Grenzen*] of his capabilities and skills.
>
> (Goethe 1998, 532, §1239; *my translation*)

A person can acquire force of character, a certain 'harmony', and even a compelling intensity if they concentrate on their potential, on what they are capable of, while respecting what is beyond their means. Goethe describes what he sees as the 'disaster' of his age, its frenetic acceleration and movement, and advocates that 'healthy people are those in whose bodily and intellectual organization each part has its own life' (Goethe 1998, §§1239, 1241). This consolidated, but also balanced and evolutive, economy of particularities involves negotiation and some compromise. However, compromise is not synonymous with resignation. On the contrary, it is a sign of ultimate strength and willpower.

Recognising one's limits [*Grenzen*] means that one avoids the risk of dissipating one's energies and running the risk of error. Kant suggests that if one believes too much in oneself, without seeking some sort of external 'proof', one carries on:

> like streams which break their banks, run wildly at random, whithersoever the current of hidden association may chance to lead them.
>
> (Kant 1983 B811)

This type of hyperactivity can be counteractive. It is important to know where we stand.

Kant warns us that we cannot know everything (the intrinsic nature of things in themselves, for instance). It is useful for us to get to know what we cannot know, where the limits to our thinking lie. However, as indicated in the above passage, we should certainly not take for granted unquestioningly anything's supposed predesignated 'usefulness'. We have a free capacity for overcoming 'every imposed limit' [*jede angegebene Grenze*] (Kant 1983, B374). This potential can be both productive and counterproductive. It encourages us to surmount 'limitations' [*Schranken*] which thwart us becoming autonomous beings. It can also encourage us to develop ourselves in directions that lead to the fruitless dissipation of our energies, hence a degree of delimitation is of critical importance. Some 'limits' [*Grenzen*] need to be set. But, as Kant makes clear in this passage, no-one 'can, or ought to' set in stone the limits [*Grenzen*] determining human nature:

> For what the highest degree may be at which mankind may have to be left between the idea and its realization, are questions which no-one can, or ought to, answer. For the issue depends on freedom; and it is in the power of freedom to pass beyond any and every imposed limit.
>
> (Kant 1983, B374)

'Limitations' [*Schranken*] are negative, whereas 'limits' [*Grenzen*] have something positive in them (Kant 1988b, 229). Kant refuses to define the limits of human nature once and for all. He thereby gives us hope that our species can evolve. However, he does also emphasise the potential strength to be gained by confronting 'limits'. He takes Plato as an example of someone who, by denigrating the phenomenal world, mistook 'limits' [*Grenzen*] for 'limitations' [*Schranken*]:

> The light dove, cleaving the air in her free flight, and feeling its resistance, might imagine that its flight would be still easier in empty space. It was thus that Plato left the world of senses, as setting too narrow limits [*Schranken*] to the understanding, and ventured out beyond it on the wings of the ideas, in the empty space of the pure understanding. He did not observe that with all his efforts he made no advance – meeting no resistance that might, as it were, serve as a support upon which he could take a stand to which he could apply his powers, and so set his understanding in motion.
>
> (Kant 1983, B8–9)

Physical constraints, that clip the wings of speculative 'free flight', are not just to be lamented. On the contrary, Kant suggests that resisting forces can vitalise and even support our projects if we work with them creatively. The same is evidently true of architecture. It is therefore not by chance that Kant continues the above passage in the following vein:

> It is, indeed, the common fate of human reason to complete its speculative structures as speedily as may be, and only afterwards to enquire whether the foundations are reliable.
>
> (Kant 1983, B9)

There might well be a place for 'castles in the sky'. Indeed, this book argues for a certain 'utopianism' in architectural thinking and doing. However, a more robust conception of what the 'utopian' means than mere speculative dreaming, without any possible basis at all in reality, would be the confrontation between theories of possible alternatives and material practice.

Testing the solidity of ideas while not 'grounding' them completely is the delicate balancing act of construction.

An architectural project where everything is possible will never exist. To be sure, money, and the invention of new technologies it can finance, can make possible structures hitherto only dreamt of. Gehry's La Fondation Louis Vuitton (discussed below) is a case in point. But in all projects there are material 'limits' at play. Paradoxically it is these very 'limits' that can open up 'playroom' [Spielraum] for architecture (Kant 1974a, 93; 1977, 544; see also Benjamin 2002, 117; 1991, 309; Elliott 2011, 122–128; and see also Kant 1988a, §§22, 23; Schiller 1982, 60–61, 94–109 for more on 'play'). The closer one hones the project to the limiting laws of construction, the riskier it can become (see Morgan 2000, 49). Reducing a structure to the barest minimum of what is needed for a building to stand, i.e. taking the law as a letter, optimising its literal application, not only lightens the building of redundant material, thereby revealing the beauty of its coordination, it also exposes it more to instability (see Vaudeville 1999).

Architects are especially well-placed to understand the stakes of Kant's critical enquiry.

Nevertheless, the discipline of architecture has often been relegated by philosophers to a sub- or almost-art form because of its accountability to 'usefulness' (Vitruvius' *utilitas*). Architectural theories and ideas are generally required to assume a more substantial form than other aesthetic disciplines. They also often have to serve a purpose. Using Kant's own politically and ethically loaded discourse, I aim to demonstrate how these very constraints [Grenzen] could be conceived as architecture's, maybe singular, opportunity to, as the grotesquely banalized expression goes, 'make a difference'. This 'difference' could even be cosmopolitical difference, as Kant requires us to envisage.

However, a lot depends on what we want from architecture. Rather than assuming what we mean by 'architecture' – especially as I suggested at the beginning, that not much architecture might be actually in evidence in these standardised times – we should seek to enquire into its specificity. We might get a keener sense of what could be expected from architecture if we compare it with other art forms. Within the history of philosophy and art, architecture's place has been an insecure one. It has often been relegated to the status of being an almost-art, too tied down by practical considerations to qualify as a 'free' medium of aesthetic expression (Hegel 1986, 294; Morgan 2000, 25–30). Paradoxically, its very groundedness has also been a characteristic that these disciplines have traditionally come to rely on, as least metaphorically as 'architectonics' ('the art of system-building') (Kant 1983, B860).

Of course architecture should not be reduced to the actual buildings that one uses. Many architectural projects do not end up standing tangibly in this world. Unbuilt and unbuildable ('utopian') projects feature as important aspects of architectural history. Especially the latter can provide a fund of stimulating ideas for future realisations. They are critical reminders that we could have constructed, and could still construct, our surroundings differently. We should therefore be on guard against tying architecture down to immediately identifiable utilitarian purposes. Kant might well agree, to some extent: it is crucial that art is not instrumentalised or commodified as it is only when aesthetic expression is autonomous that it can create beautiful spaces for us to explore ideas freely. Such 'playspaces', to use Walter Benjamin's term *Spielraum*, might even inspire alternative forms of communitarian living. We will be exploring such eventualities in Chapters 3 and 4.

However, as I have already suggested, a lot depends on how one wants to situate architecture as an art form.

What is distinctive about architecture compared to other visual arts?

A major difference is probably its relation to temporality, evoked earlier. Whether a building's function and thereby appearance, even structure, changes or not, the original project is still accountable to time in ways that other aesthetic media maybe are not. Even if reduced to a sublime sculptural ruin, the reason for its partial destruction – whether due to advanced age or because of a structural fault – counts greatly. We expect architecture to weather well, to withstand temporality to some extent so that we can use it. 'Use' might not necessitate a construction's capacity to accommodate an identified function. 'Use' might just mean that we can enter it for a brief moment or a longer period of time without it caving in on us. However, usually we do more than just enter into architecture as if it were a mere indifferent or fragile shell. Compared with other art forms, architecture is subjected to more wear and tear; we can touch its walls, even if it is a medieval castle or a Gothic cathedral, whereas its contents (e.g. furniture, paintings and sculptures) are often haptically out of bounds. Our bodies use and abuse buildings.

We can feel so at home in architecture that we do not really see it as such. We often take it for granted. We rely on it being there. That is why it might not be art ...

As we saw at the beginning of this chapter, Kant advocated that 'cultural progress' entailed putting our 'knowledge and skill' to the 'world's use', while not taking for granted what 'usefulness' is. Kant grounded his enlightened vision of critical philosophy's popular mission with an architectural metaphor: that of the house. It is an obvious image to evoke. Down-to-earth domesticity. A basic building that satisfies fundamental human needs. The familiar house locates architecture very squarely in the 'real world'. Everyone knows what a house is. Don't they?

Having laid out how and why his critical philosophy necessitates the ostensibly negative disciplining of reason (rather than its more affirmative excitation), Kant has forewarned us about the modest scale of his philosophical system. He claims that his project is not comparable to a foolhardy tower that aims to scrape the skies. Nevertheless, he does risk assumptions, which 'we' probably share, about what a house is. In the *Critique of Pure Reason* he writes:

> If we look upon the sum of all knowledge of pure speculative reason as an edifice for which we have at least the idea within ourselves, it can be said that in the Transcendental Doctrine of Elements we have made an estimate of the materials, and have determined for what sort of edifice and for what height and strength of building they suffice. We have found, indeed, that although we had contemplated building a tower which should reach to the heavens, the supply of materials only for a dwelling-house, just sufficiently roomy for our business on the level of experience, and just sufficiently high to allow of our overlooking it. The bold undertaking that we had designed is thus bound to fail through lack of material – not to mention the babel of tongues, which inevitably gives rise to disputes among the works in regard to the plan to be followed, and which must end by dispersing them over all the world, leaving each to building according to his own design. At present, however, we are concerned not so much with the materials as with the plan; and inasmuch as we have been warned not to venture at random upon a blind project which may be altogether beyond our capacities, and yet cannot well abstain from building a secure home for ourselves, we must plan our building with regard to the material which is given to us, and which is also at the same time appropriate to our needs.
>
> (Kant 1983, B735)

Despite not being a tower, Kant's 'dwelling house' still has height. It rises up, away from the ground. It is also solid and fixed. Already these characteristics preclude other architectural forms, other cultures, as we will now see in the following two sections. In a third section, we will then consider his comparison between the house and the tower.

Does a house necessarily stand?

Not everyone's house is elevated as Kant assumes: for instance, the interior spaces of underground cave dwellings (troglodytes) are thoroughly habitable rooms, but they are not buildings according to the *Oxford English Dictionary*'s definition of the term: i.e. 'that which is built ... an edifice ... a structure of the nature of a house built where it is to stand'. A 'building' is the result of the action 'to build'. This verb means: 'to erect a building ... to construct by fitting together separate parts'. Troglodytes are not erected and do not have structures: 'mutually connected and dependent elements' have not been arranged or organised into a system to produce them. While the interior spaces have volume, the troglodytes themselves have no height, just depth. They are either carved horizontally into the rock (e.g. at Douiret in Tunisia), or vertically down into the rock (as is the case in Matmata). It is 'architecture by subtraction' or 'sculpted architecture' (Rudofsky 1964, figs 14–16, 22–25).

Unobtrusive, indeed often invisible from afar, such 'anonymous' architecture is respectfully, even 'peacefully', integrated into its environment. Rudofsky argues that they '[fit] ... into the natural surroundings, instead of trying to "conquer" nature' (Rudofsky 1964). These dwellings are both ecological and economical: they do not use up materials but rather transform rock, that would otherwise just feature as an inert base or backdrop, into a living space. They are quite flexible; if more storage space is needed, extra cavities can be created without any material addition. Cool in summer and warm in the winter, they utilise the naturally tempered ventilation of the mountains themselves. Mountains breathe. In hot climates it is sensible to live in them. In erected buildings, which expose themselves by reaching out to the skies, one tends to overheat. Equally, when it cools down, it also makes sense to take advantage of the heat stored by the mountain during the day that it subsequently gradually releases, instead of reactively trying to warm up one's vulnerable edifice with artificial means.

If a person is called a 'troglodyte' in our 'civilised' times, it is not usually intended as a compliment. The term designates 'a person who lives in seclusion,

Douiret, Tunisia (horizontally excavated troglodytes).

Matmata, Tunisia (descending troglodytes).

unacquainted with the affairs of the world; a "hermit" ... a person who lives in a hovel or slum; one considered to be like a prehistoric cave-dweller' (*OED*). Such a definition is not only prejudicial, but also historically inaccurate. In Douiret, for instance, 600 families lived together until 1974 before the community gradually disintegrated when people moved to the valley into new buildings with 'mod cons' – such as air-conditioning, that was much needed down there as the stand-alone constructions baked in the heat. By contrast, rather than indicating an unsophisticated and backward way of life, troglodytes – both the caves and their dwellers – demonstrated, for Rudofsky, 'rare good sense in the handling of practical problems'. Not only were caves *per se* 'man's earliest shelters', but Rudofsky, adopting the rather apocalyptic tone of the nuclear Cold War, suggests they 'may turn out to be his last ones' (Rudolsky 1964). Rudofsky felt the need to 'break down our narrow concepts of the art of building by introducing the unfamiliar world of nonpedigreed architecture'. The broadening our conception of modes of living he deemed necessary, not only for our long-term survival, but also for a good life. Indeed the guiding idea behind his 1965 exhibition 'Architecture without Architects' was that:

> the philosophy and know-how of the anonymous builders presents the largest untapped source of architectural inspiration for industrial man. The wisdom to be derived goes beyond economic and aesthetic considerations, for it touches the far tougher and increasingly troublesome problem of how to live and let live, how to keep peace with one's neighbours, both in the parochial and universal sense.
>
> (Rudofsky 1964)

Rudofsky detected a crisis in the 'art of living'. He partially blamed architects for the impoverishment of our capacity to dwell, suggesting that they were mostly 'concerned with problems of business and prestige'. Hence, back in the 1960s, he already keenly felt the negative impact that commercialism, including tourism, was having on the quality of contemporary architecture and on the environment as a whole. I suggested earlier that this state of affairs is most topical for us today. Rudofsky considered that, in contrast to market-driven architectural practice, including what we now call 'starchitecture', the creative, organic qualities of 'nonpedigreed' or 'communal architecture' was in 'connivance with nature'. Paradoxically he therefore viewed its guiding concepts as 'verg[ing] on the utopian' and its aesthetics as 'approach[ing] the sublime'. Far from being backward-looking, he regarded this architecture as providing models for a more ideal future, both more ecologically sustainable and more communitarian. This objective is also Kant's. As this book will repeatedly demonstrate,

<u>building for a better future is precisely Kant's sublime</u> <u>'cosmopolitical' project. It is one that those engaged with</u> <u>architectural theory and practice can, and should,</u> <u>contribute to.</u>

Is a house necessarily solid and fixed?

Kant assumes, as 'we' probably do, that to provide proper shelter, to be comfortable and 'roomy', a house has to have solid walls that are reassuringly anchored in the ground. However, this assumption is also open to discussion. For nomadic cultures the very idea of a permanently sedentary life might signify discomfort. Not everyone wants to be tied to one place. Once again, this issue is not a minor one. One just has to consider the place that mobile architecture holds, not only in other cultures but in also in our own. Many experimental, 'utopian' projects (like those of Archigram, e.g. Michael Webb's Suitaloon, David Greene's 'living pod', Ron Herron's 'walking city'; or of the Utopie group, e.g. Jean Aubert, Jean-Paul Jungmann, Antoine Stinco's 'Pneumatic Living-Economical Mobile') consist of easily transportable, modifiable structures that enable their inhabitants to lead freer, more independent and yet more 'open' lives than those of sedentarians.

Inflatable suit-home, final stage of the sequence of the suit being inflated from Package to Home; David Greene (suit made by Pat Haines based on the Suitaloon project by Michael Webb (1968).

Having the potential to be always on the move can produce a different mindset, less materialistic and defensive, more expansive and communitarian, than those who enclose themselves in closeted spaces. Of course, one might well be living in a temporary construction, such as a tent, due to a natural or man-made disaster. It could be because one is poor, a refugee or a migrant worker. If this is the case, having a 'secure home' that is 'appropriate to [one's] needs' is not to be snubbed (see Kant 1983, B735). However, to imagine a more positive scenario, tents and other portable structures are also a useful means for enabling people to form makeshift communities, often around a shared conviction or passion (e.g. peace camps, musical festivals, etc.). In these latter instances, one could even feel more 'at home' in these alternative places during exceptional times than back in one's more conventional house (where more staid relations are likely to be in place). The experiences one has in these tents might even generate new ideas about how to lead one's life, or even reorganise society as a whole. Given that we have already alluded to Kant's 'utopian' hope that sometime in the future we will lead 'universal cosmopolitan existence[s]', these reflections about the various guises 'houses' take in other cultures are not frivolous. They demonstrate that Kant's down-to-earth example of the modest house is less self-evident and more interesting than it might have at first appeared.

Reaching for the skies: building the tower and multivocality

In the book of the Christian Bible 'Genesis', the world originally created by the Lord was claimed to be 'of one language and of one speech':

> Let us build us a city and a tower, whose top *may reach* unto heaven; and let us make us a name, lest we be scattered abroad upon the face of the whole earth.
>
> (Genesis 11, 4)

This gift was then abused when it became the means by which a collective building project was decided upon without divine permission. Having considered that humankind had overstepped the mark with their Tower of Babel, God punishes them for their hubris: henceforth they will speak different languages, frustrating any easy communication between them. These linguistic barriers in turn lead to the breaking up of the single unified society; humans are dispersed over the surface of the earth to live in different, smaller communities, rendering any future universally shared project difficult.

In the passage from *Critique of Pure Reason* cited above, Kant revisits this biblical story. Describing his critical project in architectonic terms, he wrote:

> The bold undertaking that we had designed is thus bound to fail through lack of material – not to mention the babel of tongues, which inevitably gives rise to disputes among the works in regard to the plan to be followed, and which must end by dispersing them over all the world, leaving each to building according to his own design.
>
> (Kant 1983, B735)

Instead of regarding the non-completion of an ambitious tower as a result of divine punishment, Kant suggests that, due to the project's very nature, it was bound to fail. How could one ever reach the heavens? They are not a destination one could ever arrive at. Building materials would necessarily run out for such an infinite project. Additionally, the construction site for such a large-scale project would require the bringing together of so many workers that already-existing cultural differences, language being one of them, would inevitably thwart the successful realisation of the grandiose vision, if there ever was originally just one. Kant was in favour of cultural difference and saw 'unsocial sociability' not only as an unavoidable aspect of the 'human condition', but also as a source of productive tension (Kant 1994, 44). Any aspiration to universality – e.g. the institution of 'human rights' – has to negotiate, work with and against potentially conflictual differences. The basic building block for his cosmopolitical project is not homogeneously solid. The babble of 'foreign tongues' is not a social ill to be eradicated; it is rather the diverse stuff of which humans are made. Kant's 'dwelling house' will have to accommodate a variety of inhabitants, whose preconceptions of what constitutes 'domesticity' differ greatly. It cannot remain hermetic but must embrace a degree of 'porosity' (to employ Benjamin's term mentioned in the Introduction).

Kant's reference to the Tower of Babel inadvertently draws our attention to the surreal character and uncanniness of building sites. They are often, if not always, cacophonously populated places. Paintings are often the work of one person.

Sculptures and photographs also sometimes are. Music, dance and film more often than not involve several if not many people, though not necessarily. It depends. By contrast,

<u>architecture practically always requires a team of people working together.</u>

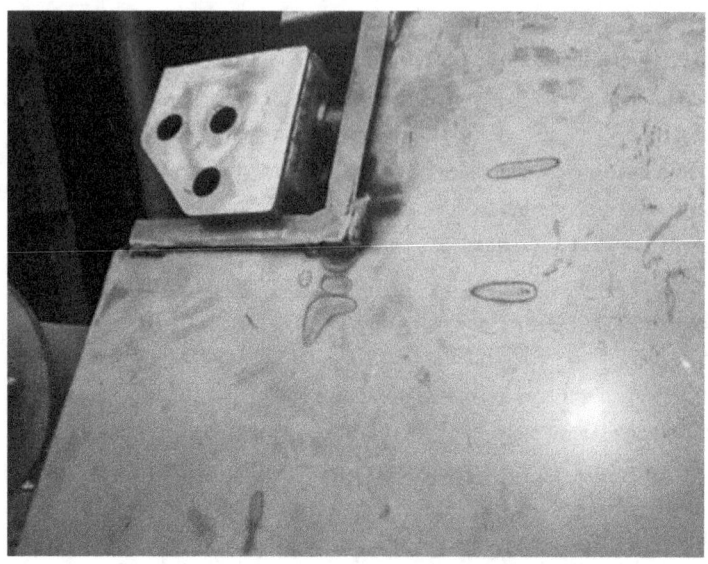

The uncanniness of the building site: La Fondation Louis Vuitton.

The building site is therefore an integral and distinctive feature of architecture.

> Nevertheless, once the plans have been successfully executed, most traces of the complicated and often chaotic building process are subsequently effaced. Thus the historical dimension of architecture's making is elided and the finished product stands artificially pristine, shorn of the colourful collective contributions that informed it. If authorship is considered to be of consequence, more often than not solely the architect's name will be acknowledged, whereas the engineer's contribution is omitted and all signs of the construction workers and their equipment are removed. The walls often become smooth and homogeneous. The extent to which the guts, muscle and organs of the building are to be left visible or not become an architect's aesthetic vision about its 'design'.

One of the colourful characters of the building site of La Fondation Louis Vuitton.

Kant's apparently straightforward description of his critical project as a modest house, as compared to the more daring tower, raises yet further issues. First, to return again to Rudofsky, towering buildings are not necessarily contentious. Rudofsky shows himself historically informed about cultural differences and critical of his times when he writes:

> Only in our time are towers built for profit and usury. In the past their significance was mainly symbolic. Apart from the functional defensive towers, they usually expressed religious sentiments – faith, hope, grief and the like. Spires, minarets and pagodas were, or are, essential parts of buildings intended for launching prayers, only the notorious Tower of Babel spelled, unaccountably, blasphemy.
>
> (Rudofsky 1964)

In contemporary society it seems that towers are increasingly featuring as spectacular symbols of corporate and state power. 'Profit and usury' attend power. Cities and nations, both established and emerging, compete to build 'megatall' towers, such as the Chinese city of Wuhan's current aim to build 900-metre-high twin towers. As a result, traditional 'modest dwelling houses' are demolished. Elsewhere the opposite phenomenon occurs: due to a reductive appraisal of modernist high-rise social housing, sprawling dormitory towns are instead built. These new towns eat into precious greenfield land. Often dependent on cars and out-of-town supermarket shopping, their residents are in effect complicit in the destruction of urban local communities and the further propagation of multinational commodity 'culture'.

<u>The scale, density and proportion of architectural projects affect our world more immediately and directly than other art forms do. Architects could therefore be deemed more especially responsible for their interventions than other artists.</u>

Prudence and vigilance are characteristics that Kant attributes to architecture and, by association, with his philosophical system. Far from not caring about how his building materials are sourced, he insists on knowing their provenance:

> Now it does seem natural that, as soon as we have left the ground of experience, we should, through careful enquiries, assure ourselves as to the foundations of any building that we propose to erect, not making use of any knowledge that we propose without first determining whence it has come, and not trusting to principles without knowing their origin.
>
> (Kant 1983, B7)

Even if various operations are subcontracted out, a Kantian architect would nevertheless feel bound to enquire as to what principles, if indeed there are any, have been put into practice on the building site. Kant makes it clear that cowboy, or cowgirl, builders who do not take their responsibilities seriously and whose prime interest is to realise their projections as quickly as possible without taking into due consideration the – social, political, environmental – impact of the ensuing edifice are not to be tolerated:

> It is indeed the common fate of human reason to complete its speculative structures as speedily as may be, and only afterwards to enquire whether the foundations are reliable. All sorts of excuses will then be appealed to, in order to reassure us of their solidity, or rather indeed to enable us to dispense altogether with so late and so dangerous an enquiry.
>
> (Kant 1983, B9)

By failing to follow through on the smaller details of the complex practice of embodying ideas in the material world, the structure of the whole edifice could be put in danger. Such an instability could literally arise in the actual process of building. However, Kant is here leaning on architecture as a powerful metaphor for the general frameworks, concepts, principles and judgements that we constantly have recourse to in our everyday lives. They serve as a means to orientate ourselves in the world, to give us a sense of direction, to create an environment that signifies something for us. It is therefore crucial that we regularly examine this artificially constructed basis to see whether it grounds our finite existences as 'solidly' (rigorously, thoroughly) as we can.

CHAPTER 3

The precarious situation of architecture and its relation to beauty

In the previous chapter, architecture featured prominently as a grounding metaphor for Kant's philosophical project. As we have seen, crucial to Kant's plan to enable us to think critically for ourselves was a sense of what is 'useful', what is intended to serve an end and, by contrast, what is counterproductive and risks dissipating our efforts to construct a positive world for ourselves. He wrote:

> With a thing that owes its possibility to a *purpose*, a building, or even an animal, its regularity, which consists in symmetry must express the unity of the intuition accompanying the concept of its end, and belongs to its cognition.
>
> (Kant 1987, §22; *my italics*)

Nevertheless, at various moments we have also questioned the drive to maximise 'usefulness'. We suggested that functionality can be over-designed, rendering a space almost uninhabitable. We might even think that a place should be accorded to what is 'frivolous', to that which flouts 'regularity' by entertaining what is not strictly necessary. A certain degree of 'excess' can not only be pleasurable in itself, but also, if the decorative ornament requires further justification, it might even paradoxically have its 'uses'. It can make our lives agreeable and meaningful. We will be exploring these ideas later on in this chapter in relation to Kant's notion of 'ornament' or the *parergon*.

Following Vitruvius, we also asserted that *venustas* (beauty), along with *utilitas* and *firmitas*, is one of the essential qualities of architecture as an art form. However, Kant here adds a dissonant voice. For him, the aesthetic pleasure that we derive from beauty is incompatible with something being conceived of as perfectly serving a use, as being fit for purpose. Beauty was associated by him with an idea of freedom that cannot be shackled by overt purposefulness (*utilitas*). Indeed, he described the beautiful as displaying 'purposiveness without purpose' (*Zweckmässigkeit ohne Zweck*) (Kant 1988a, §15). The pleasingly co-ordinated composition and exquisite (tactile, acoustic, visual, rhythmic) qualities of the object might be sensed by us to be 'perfect', but this cannot mean that it aptly corresponds to 'what it is supposed to be'. If this were the case, it would be determined by a finality external to it; it would not be free. Kant illustrates what he means with a touchingly quaint example of forest clearings and country dancing. He begins by detaching the apparent unified 'perfection' or 'purposiveness' of an object (in this case the clearing) from any 'purpose' or 'end':

> For since abstraction is made from this unity as end (what the thing is to be) nothing is left but the subjective finality of the representations in the mind of the Subject intuiting ... For instance, if in a forest I light upon a plot of grass, round which trees stand in a circle, and if I do not then form any representation of an end, as that it is meant to be used, say, for country dances, then not the least hint of a concept of perfection is given by the mere form.
>
> (Kant 1988a, §15)

The scenario Kant depicts is an evocative one: we can well imagine traversing a dark, damp forest, tripping over brittle branches, getting caught in the prickly and stinging undergrowth, until we finally break out into a light-flooded clearing where the sun's rays provide a warming contrast to what we have left behind. Animated, morally and physically, by this miraculously verdant sight and site, we are understandably prompted to strip off our by now unnecessary layers of clothing and have a celebratory jig. Indeed, the place seems ideally designed for such a purpose. However, by attributing a function or 'end' to this beautiful place, we detract from the miraculous wondrousness of its beauty.

Kant's wish to preserve beauty from what is 'purposive' or has utilitas, has important consequences, especially for architecture.

The result is its precarious situation within his philosophy. Its usefulness makes it at once central to his project metaphorically, yet this same down-to-earth functionality detracts from its status as art. It risks being relegated by Kant to a subordinate art form whose formal constraints tend to compromise autonomous aesthetic expression, in ways that do not apply to other, more 'liberal' art forms, such as poetry, painting, theatre and music. The beauty offered by architecture would be merely 'adherent' or 'appendant', not 'free' or 'pure'. The potential for architecture to create 'playspace', an experimental alternative time–space zone wherein the 'utopian' potential of the aesthetic can be explored, would thereby be compromised. We will now examine Kant's ambivalent treatment of architecture in more depth.

Architecture: too down-to-earth to be beautiful?

For Kant, beauty strikes the eye 'immediately' (Kant 1988a, §16). At that moment in time, considerations about what beauty might mean, or what use it is, are irrelevant. They do not interest us. However, when it comes to architecture, the 'purity' of the aesthetic encounter runs the risk of being parasited. Hence Kant asserts that:

> Much might be added to a building that would immediately please the eye, were it not meant to be a church.
>
> (Kant 1988a, §16)

For Kant, architecture is all too often tied down by considerations of functionality [*utilitas*], and these get in the way of our spontaneous appreciation of its aesthetic form. The designated use of a building is seen as determining what the end-product will be. The architectural work of art is thereby captured: it risks being reduced to the effect of a cause. Its 'perfection' as a finished product has to be in line with the animating concept or intention that informs it. As such, the architectural object resembles more the mere execution of an act, or the resulting effect of an operation. Kant employs the verbs *Handeln*, *Wirken* and *agere* to suggest a form of making that he consider to be less creative than a freer doing of things (for which he uses the terms *Tun or facere*) (Kant 1988a, §43). In this scenario, builders are like bees programmed to construct honeycombs. Equally, their work could also resemble that of craftsmen, as defined by Kant. That is to say, it is 'industrial' or 'mercenary' art [*Lohnkunst*], resulting from work that is in itself 'disagreeable' (unpleasant and hard), and whose compensation is financial return. Any ensuing aesthetic qualities are to be attributed less to genial talent, and more to a well-designed manufacturing process and diligently acquired know-how.

However, when we look at Kant's *Critique of Judgement* more closely, we see that his analysis is far more intriguing. His hesitations about the place of architecture as an art form pertinently draw our attention to issues that bear on contemporary debates about who produces, and indeed what constitutes, 'good' construction. To begin with: who do we consider to be the creator(s) of architecture? If architectural projects can be artistic compositions or '*oeuvres*' (*opus*) – to return to Lefebvre's distinction between 'works' and 'products' mentioned earlier – who authors them? We have already suggested that all too often the finished building gets solely attributed to the architect(s), and the contributions made by the majority of the team, the engineers and contractors, are effaced. Kant's use of the architectonic as a metaphor for his own system-building as a philosopher, seems likewise to attribute the edifice to the controlling intention of an architect, or possibly to a structural engineer, upon whom it is wholly incumbent to assure the solidity and security of the foundations and who is responsible for trying and testing the 'principles' being implemented for the construction (Kant 1983, B7). However, we also considered earlier the attention he paid the multi-headed building site crew, whose differences inevitably interfere with even the most dogmatically implemented 'plan', and whose personalities are far more distinctive than that of drones who instinctively carry out orders (Kant 1983, B735).

In this same section of *Critique of Judgement* (§43), Kant gives what we might consider to be a reductive reading of craft. We might well balk at the definition of 'craft' as '*Lohnkunst*' (i.e. a type of sub-'art' quasi-mechanically carried out for pecuniary reasons) for many reasons, one being because it could also, by implication, apply to architecture. All depends again on whether we consider the actual builders of architecture to be 'mercenaries' who have 'purposively' sold themselves to be the 'means' by which someone else's projected end is carried out in conditions that are often 'disagreeable' (to refer back to Kant's definition in 1988a, §43). To be sure, building sites are indeed often filthy, dangerous, tiring, noisy places. However, as was suggested earlier, they are also vitally energetic, marvellous and admirable, places where heroically transformative work is performed.

Indeed, building sites can understandably capture the popular imagination. Site-workers can really make the earth move! For a passer-by, it is sometimes shocking to come across an enormous building site that lays bare a gap in the normally dense and confining urban fabric. Walter Benjamin, cited earlier, described our urban environment as a 'prison world'. When we encounter a building site, what one had habitually taken to be solidly 'there', has suddenly disappeared and what was previously hidden also emerges as the entrails of the streets and roads around the new construction are ripped open to serve its growing needs.

The building site can unexpectedly put the stability of our lives into question and even permanently undermine the very foundations of traditional beliefs and societal relations.

As William Golding so well describes in his compelling novel about Salisbury Cathedral, *The Spire*, regardless of how spiritually motivated one presumes the initial aesthetic intentions to be, the actual materialisation of the idea pollutes its purported purity. Golding's Dean Jocelin, whose inspiration it is to erect a glorious spire, is appalled by the workplace that his project engenders. He exclaims: 'the place is filthy dirty! They dirty everything' (Golding 2005, 60). Jocelin later realises that the 'corruption' of his vision is in fact not the fault of shoddy workmen, but that it lies within the very processes of conceptualisation and making. He acknowledges to Roger, the master-builder, that:

> When such a work is ordained, it is put into the mind of a, of a man. That's a terrible thing. I'm only learning now, how terrible it is. It's a refiner's fire. The man knows little of the purpose; but nothing of the cost – *why* can't they keep quiet out there? *Why* don't they stand quietly and wait? No. You and I were chosen to do this thing together. It's a great glory. I see that it'll destroy us of course. What are we, after all? Only I tell you this, Roger; with the whole strength of my soul. The thing can be built and will be built, in the very teeth of Satan.
>
> (Golding 2005, 88)

Like the common paid workers, the Dean himself might have sold his soul to the devil.

Nevertheless, Kant's term 'mercenary art' is probably an inadequate way to describe the creativity involved in construction, considered as an instance of 'craft'. Indeed, if we think that all forms of craftsmanship are far more than an unthinkingly carried out form of manual work, we will need to highlight the complexities and innovative skills involved in manual work. Too often questionable assumptions are made about the mind–body relation. As we know, binary oppositions often operate in practice as hierarchical power relations. In this case, instead of the apparent opposition between two equal forces, 'mind' is generally privileged over 'body' (just as 'male' tends to be over 'female', and 'white' over 'black'). Maybe it is a sign of our highly technologised times that the relation between physicality and the intellect is being re-evaluated? However, we probably have always felt uneasy and unsure about their supposed differences and similarities. In *The Case for Working With Your Hands*, Matthew Crawford recently argued that 'getting an adequate grasp on the world, intellectually, depends on getting a handle on it in some literal and active sense' (Crawford 2009, 7). Crawford, for one, considers that our present world of digital technology has led to the decline of tool use, with the result that we have become increasingly dependent and passive as human beings, less intellectually alive, and so more materially impoverished. For Crawford, manipulating a computer mouse would be a 'poorer' experience than using a pencil on paper to design a building. Crawford describes his experience as an electrician, whose work often leaves no visible trace once the building has been completed, or the repair job carried out, in the following way:

> As a residential and light-commercial electrician, most of my work got covered up inside walls. Still, I felt pride in meeting the aesthetic demands of a workmanlike installation. Maybe another electrician would see it someday. Even if not, I felt responsible to my better self. Or rather, to the thing itself – craftsmanship has been said to consist simply in the desire to do something well, for its own sake. If the primary satisfaction is intrinsic and private in this way, there is nonetheless a sort of self-disclosing that takes place.
>
> (Crawford 2009, 14)

Having earlier drawn our attention to the abuses of the economically (and therefore socially, and sometimes legally and politically) precarious situation of many manual labourers on building sites, I am far from wanting to romanticise this type of work at all costs. Hence, if we bear in mind the catastrophic effects of 'uneven geography' for many lives on this planet, our interest in such recent re-evaluations of 'craft' must accompany a more general topical debate about the nature of work. If work can be a potentially creative process that can positively affect not only those individuals directly employed, but society as a whole, the assurance of positive working conditions for all should be everyone's concern.

In his contribution to the re-evaluation of the place of 'craft', Glenn Adamson has eloquently suggested that 'it' is less the production of 'a fixed set of things – pots, rather than paintings' and more 'an approach, an attitude, or a habit of action'. He continues to unfurl the various aspects of 'craft' as 'process' in the following passage from *Thinking Through Craft*:

> Craft only exists in motion. It is a way of doing things, not a classification of objects, institutions, or people. It is also multiple: an amalgamation of interrelated core principles, which are put into relation with one another through the overreaching idea of 'craft'.
>
> (Adamson 2007, 5)

Accordingly, in a chapter on skill, Adamson considers craft as the sophisticated management of risk. One of his examples of master-craftsmen is Tilman Riemenschneider (c.1460–1531), whose sculptures in lime-wood are seen to testify to a cultural respect for the material being handled. Indeed, Riemenschneider's works have been read as manifestations of a principled attitude, modest, unassuming but nevertheless strongly resistant to injustices, a stance indicative of certain aspects of the German Reformation (MacGregor 2014, 213–229). It becomes clear that craftsmanship can reveal a whole way of, and approach to, life. Adamson follows this discussion with a presentation of 'inductive experiences of doing' as theorised and practised by Josef Albers at the Bauhaus and then at Black Mountain College. Albers' 'open-ended pedagogy' was based, not so much on the transmission of knowledge from master to pupil with (to use contemporary jargon) preset 'aims and objectives' and 'learning outcomes' in mind, but more on the creation of situations wherein students could experience and actively explore 'material contingencies'. For Albers, the learning process at the alternatively minded institutions of Dessau and North Carolina therefore went well beyond the acquisition of a specific *content*; it was also the enlivening of a *form* of 'utopian' communitarianism.

It is after his discussion of Albers' experimental theories and practice that architecture makes its appearance in Adamson's book. While still considering the topic of skill, Adamson suggests that one might think that architecture 'would be the last discipline' in which one might look for a continuation of his previous discussions, given that up to now he had been concerned with a 'celebration of open-ended exploration, an engagement with materials that may result in "readiness" in the mind, but nothing in the way of a product'. The reason for his assumption is that '[architects] care most about getting their work built'. He continues:

> They may engage in speculation of both theoretical and visual varieties, and certainly the archives of architectural libraries worldwide are stuffed with images of unrealised projects. But in the end architecture must contend with the challenge of shaping the world in the most concrete, political sense.
>
> (Adamson 2007, 87)

Once again we appear to return to Kant's image of architecture as a project that has to end up being firmly based and functioning in the now. Architecture is preconceived as being 'goal orient[ed]'. However, Adamson then picks as his examples 'DIY' or 'ad hoc' architecture that foregrounds the processes that not only inform it, but give it form, a form that is still being defined. Indeed, it is as if the constructions are still being made, or will never finish being made, preferring instead to remain open-ended, and thereby responsive to the changing needs and desires of their inhabitants. Such constructions can also be indicative of a particular political stance, one concerned with recuperation and recycling, making a place habitable, and even expressive, out of what in consumer culture is wasted and neglected. As such these constructions can be critical of dominant trends.

Among the examples given by Adamson of this sort of self-built architecture (drawing on the so-called postmodern theories of Charles Jencks) are the early projects of Gehry. He writes:

> The lack of craftsmanship in such buildings became a point of pride in itself, and propagated a down-at-heel aesthetic that was imitated by sculptors as well as professional architects. Jencks approved of this development, later writing that the 'approximate craftsmanship' of Californian woodbutchers, the example of their 'improvisation, creativity, incongruity and iconic imagery' was crucial in the formation of leading architects such as Frank Gehry and Eric Owen Moss.
>
> (Adamson 2007, 89).

Earlier on we evoked Gehry as a starchitect who was hardly likely to build a Guggenheim in Kaliningrad, in what was Kant's Königsberg, and I later referred to Gehry again when examining Kant's metaphor of the modest dwelling house for his down-to-earth critical project. Kant warned us against the dangers to which speculative towers exposed themselves. For him they were doomed to failure because of their sheer scale, which necessitates an inordinately concerted mobilisation of manpower and resources for their realisation. We then used the occasion provided by Kant to first reflect on the nature of building sites. The example of Gehry's recent Fondation Louis Vuitton was evoked to draw attention to how these highly charged places, where the raw processes that go into a construction's making become action, are mainly effaced on completion and if partially retained, packaged as an authored 'design' choice on the part of the architect. Re-encountering Gehry here, in the context of self-built houses and 1960s–1970s counterculture, is challenging given our previous association of him with the luxury of designer labels and consumerist 'culture'. We might have to complexify our analysis of his work. In any case, Kant's analysis of beauty in the third *Critique* will oblige us to do so.

What does beauty care about?

In his *Critique of Judgement*, Kant writes:

> If anyone asks me whether I consider that the palace I see before me is beautiful, I may, perhaps, reply that I do not care for things of that sort that are merely made to be gaped at. Or I may reply in the same strain as that Iroquois *sachem* who said that nothing in Paris pleased him better than the eating-houses. I may even go a step further and inveigh with the vigour of a *Rousseau* against the vanity of the great who spend the sweat of the people on such superfluous things. Or, in fine, I may quite persuade myself that I found myself on an uninhabited island, without hope of ever again coming among men, and could conjure such a splendid edifice into existence by a mere wish, I should still not trouble to do so, so long

as I had a hut there that was comfortable enough for me. All this may be admitted and approved; only it is not the point now at issue.

(Kant 1988a, §2)

Up to now we identified Kant as a rigorously ethical thinker. He was seen to demand constant responsibility for our actions from us. He was presented as claiming that we should always take into consideration just how situated our activities are within a network of relations, and that we should always remain accountable to the wider consequences of everything we do, and do not do. However, in this passage it seems that none of these ethical and political concerns matter when it comes to finding something beautiful. It is suggested that

aesthetic pleasure doesn't give a damn for how much a building cost, what it is intended to be, who built it and why.

Not only does this proposition, with its example of the palace, seem to contradict his point, discussed earlier (Kant 1988a, §16), that architecture cannot deliver examples of free beauty as functionality always predetermines its projects. It also seems to justify the most spectacular examples of architectural luxury [*Prachtgebäude*] that could be entirely dependent on consumer 'culture' and are therefore complicit with the raw inequalities this type of economy propagates and the false – socially toxic – values it promotes. It was exactly this type of moral irresponsibility that Kant's work seemed to condemn.

Hence it is somewhat shocking to read, in the above passage, Kant's dismissal of the well-meaning moraliser, who criticises the beautiful for being just a superficial spectacle that manipulates our affects, as having completely missed the point. Apparently for Kant, the beautiful *should* be simply stared at in admiration. Equally inappropriate for Kant is the reaction of the tourist who prefers to spend his time in restaurants as a way of getting to know

Parisian culture, rather than visiting the city's famous monuments. He, too, has apparently failed to understand the significance of beauty. By comparing the beautiful unfavourably with the culinary art, however *haute*, he has associated it with the sensuous, with what can at most be agreeable. The beautiful is placed elsewhere by Kant, out of reach of those with a penchant for gluttony. The same goes for the politically rigorous critic, who cuts short any aesthetic enjoyment of the beautiful with right-on reflections about the class system and the edifice's financial, social, cultural, ecological and political cost. He is also wasting his breath with Kant. Those who profess indifference towards grandiose palaces, preferring a plain hut that adequately services basic needs also do not fare any better. All such 'critical and cynical' utterances are ruled out as irrelevant when appreciating the beautiful. How can Kant possibly dare say this? Should we not practice moderation in all things and not lust after what is excessive, what is not strictly necessary? Is Kant now preciously defending art for art's sake? Does anything go so long as it is 'beautiful', even if, especially if, we don't need it? Kant now appears to be encouraging us to renege on our moral and political responsibilities. It leaves us wondering what exactly the nature of the beautiful might be. Can it possibly be thought of as potentially creative of utopian 'playspace', as Kant earlier seemed to suggest, if it is political irresponsible, or at least doesn't directly care about social issues?

The beautiful, the utopian dream and the 'real' world of consumer culture

Kant defines 'free beauty' as what pleases by its own accord, independent of any purpose or concept that would otherwise have to be served. '[F]lowers, parrots, humming-birds, birds of paradise and a lot of crustaceans in the sea ... designs *à la grecque*, the foliage on borders or on wallpapers ... fantasias in music' are some of his intriguing, if somewhat disconcerting, examples (Kant 1987, §16). By contrast, buildings (he names churches, palaces, arsenals and garden houses) and, most controversially, horses are instances of 'adherent' or 'dependent' beauty for him as they have a 'purpose' (Kant 1987, §16). They have to serve particular human needs and this function predetermines them. The questions I would therefore like to ask are as follows: can a building such as La Fondation Louis Vuitton be a 'free beauty', or does it serve a purpose (as does

La Fondation Louis Vuitton, Paris. Other excellent photographs of La Fondation Louis Vuitton have been taken by Yves Marchand and Romain Meffre. In 2010 these photographers produced a stunning publication of sublime images of post-industrial Detroit, a very different topic from La Fondation Louis Vuitton, and one that raises issues relating to the nefarious effects of consumer culture and global capitalism. Nevertheless, in their more recent work, while deploring the 'standardisation of the [contemporary] urban paysage', Marchant and Meffre consider Gehry's project to be a 'rare example of a building that has not been sterilised'. They add: 'Today one has to have a patron like LVMH in order to produce a beautiful building that is a symbol of power and radiance' (cited by Odey 2014, 179).

> most architecture)? If so, which one(s)? My reasons for singling out this building are twofold: first, Gehry himself has already featured prominently in discussions about architecture's relation to use and spectacle (see Vidler 2008); second, La Fondation Louis Vuitton has itself already been hailed by some as a landmark building for the twenty-first century, at the very least. Indeed its patron, Bernard Arnault, considers that it is a 'foundational act' of monumental and utopian value, not only for the city of Paris but for all citizens of the world, both those actually living now and those yet to be born (*Connaissances des arts* 2014b, 5).

In a longer version of the same article entitled 'A Dream Become Reality', he accordingly asserts that:

> The Foundation goes beyond the ephemeral; it reflects a veritable force of optimism. It also shows a passion for liberty. It is a dream become reality ... Picasso's words occur to me, words that in effect have inspired us throughout our project: 'art serves to wash the soul of the dust of everyday life'. Enthusiasm must be stimulated because enthusiasm is what we need most for ourselves and for future generations.
>
> (*Fondation Louis Vuitton Le Journal* 2014, 1; *my translation*)

Such vast claims merit being tested. By so doing, we will necessarily be discussing the utopian function of the beautiful in architecture, specifically within the current neoliberal climate, using Kant as our philosophical guide.

As is well-known, Bernard Arnault is the chairman of Louis Vuitton Moët Hennessey (LVMH). This many-tentacled group includes makers of posh bags (an acquired taste in all meanings of the term), belts, and chests, as well as champagne and cognac, fashion, cosmetics and perfumes (i.e. Dior). In short, luxury items that lay claim to traditional craftsmanship (a topic we have recently evoked, but in a completely different context). Arnault is the richest person in France, and the tenth richest in the world. His patronage of the arts – and that of others like him – includes the now generally practised private sponsorship of exhibitions in state-run museums.

The erosion of the power of public institutions and the increasing commodification of art by the art market is a sign of our times and the source of much controversy in which architecture is now inextricably implicated.

Indeed, since the opening of the Bilbao Guggenheim in 1997, Frank Gehry, one of the most 'successful' architects on the planet, stands at the centre of this debate. The recent inauguration of his La Fondation Louis Vuitton is a crystallisation of many pressing issues about the meaning and destination of architecture as a discipline and art form today.

In an article entitled 'The Triumph of Utopia', Jean-Paul Claverie, Arnault's adviser, describes the working relations between those involved in the project in the most ideal of terms:

> I want to stress the rare quality of the human relation that Frank wanted to forge with everyone involved in the project. These words of Frank's say everything: '*If you are happy, it makes me happy*' ... A true closeness was fostered between [Bernard Arnault and Frank Gehry] and between the two teams that enabled this utopian project to see the day.
>
> (*Connaissances des arts* 2014b, 11)

Of course it is important for architects to make their client 'happy', but whether serving their interests makes everyone happy remains to be seen. For writer John Ruskin and designer-maker and essayist William Morris, happiness in labour was a highly politically charged issue. In his preface to the Kelmscott edition of Ruskin's *The Nature of the Gothic*, Morris wrote:

> For the lesson which Ruskin here teaches us is that art is the expression of man's pleasure in labour; that it is possible for man to rejoice in his work, for, strange as it may seem to us to-day, there have been times when he did rejoice in it; and lastly, that unless man's work once again becomes a pleasure to him, the token of which change will be that beauty is once again a natural and necessary accompaniment of productive labour, all but the worthless must toil in pain and therefore live in pain. So that the result of the thousands of years of man's effort on the earth must be general unhappiness and universal degradation ... If Politics are to be anything else than an empty game, more exciting but less innocent than those which are confessedly

games of skill or chance, it is toward this goal of the happiness of labour that they must make.

(Morris in Ruskin 2011, i–ii)

Following in Ruskin's wake, Morris makes it clear how happiness at work can be a crucially political affair. Ruskin had advocated that Gothic architecture permitted the workmen more freedom of expression than other styles and periods (e.g. Greek and Egyptian) owing to its 'perpetual change both in design and execution' (Ruskin 2011, 34). In *The Seven Lamps of Architecture*, the question of whether the building work was carried out with 'enjoyment', or not, is considered to be the decisive factor for judging the quality of the ornament of edifices. The 'happiness' with which even the hardest work is carried out determines whether the result is 'living' or not (Ruskin 1988, 173). It makes itself visible in the 'imperfections' and 'deviations' of the details, sure signs of creative initiative having been taken by the handworkers. Should we now return to Claverie's claim that 'Frank' wanted to make everyone happy and test its 'authenticity', to decide how much of what he says is sheer PR discourse that mars our appreciation of the building, and how much is historic 'truth'? Before we do so, let us consider what Kant would say.

Going on what we know already of *Critique of Judgement*, we would probably have to admit that Kant would maintain that such an enquiry – albeit well-meaning, critically vigilant, politically 'right-on', etc. – is totally beside the point when it comes to judging a building aesthetically. For him, if we deem something to be beautiful, our judgement cannot be determined as a fulfilment of any sort of constraining criteria. Maybe Ruskin is right; testimonial evidence of the happy 'life and accent' of the worker's creative hand might well be a factor in our finding something beautiful. Nevertheless, regardless of how rigorous and purposive our definition of 'happiness' is, it does not necessarily have its place in aesthetic judgement. For Kant, 'happiness' conjures up a sensual well-being, even if our advocacy for its social value is admirably politically and spiritually motivated. For Kant, the beautiful occupies a space that is supposed to be separate from what is agreeable and what is considered to be good (morally true and honest, politically right or just). This radical separation of the beautiful from the interests of the agreeable and the good is clearly stated in the following passages from the *Critique of Judgment*:

> *Delight* in the agreeable *is coupled with interest.*
>
> *That is agreeable which the senses find pleasing in sensation* ... a judgment on an object by which its agreeableness is affirmed, expresses an interest in it, is evident from the fact that through sensation it provokes a desire for similar objects ... Hence we do not merely say of the agreeable that it *pleases*, but that it *gratifies*. I do not accord it a simple approval, but inclination is aroused by it, and where agreeableness is of the liveliest type a judgment on the character of the Object is so entirely out of place, that those who are always intent only on enjoyment (for that is the word used to denote intensity or gratification) would fain dispense with all judgment.
>
> (Kant 1988a, §3)

We want what is agreeable to us. We can even crave it. We do not even pretend to be objective about our thinking of the object as agreeable. We want it for ourselves, and we do not necessarily wish to share it with others. For Kant, we aren't here talking about what is beautiful.

The same case applies to the 'good'. Kant writes:

> *Delight* in the good *is coupled with interest.*
>
> That is good which by means of reason commends itself by its mere concept. We call that *good for something* (useful) which only pleases as a means; but that which pleases on its own account we call *good in itself*. In both cases the concept of an end is implied, and consequently the relation of reason to (at least possible) willing and thus a delight in the *existence* of an Object or action i.e. some interest or other. To deem something good, I must always know what sort of thing the object is intended to be, i.e. I must have a concept of it. That is not necessary to enable me to see

beauty in a thing. Flowers, free patterns, lines aimlessly intertwining –
technically termed foliage – have no signification, depend upon no definite
concept, and yet please. Delight in the beautiful must depend upon the
reflection on an object precursory to some (not definitely determined)
concept. It is thus also differentiated from the agreeable, which rests
entirely upon sensation.

(Kant 1988a, §4)

When we have deemed something to be 'good', we have either determined it as a useful means to an end, or identified it conceptually as something good in itself, that it might be in our interest to aspire to, or to implement as a principle. Whatever the case may be, the beautiful either resists such instrumentalisation, or is destroyed by it. The beautiful is not to be press-ganged into serving what is of 'interest' to us, however well-meaning. Kant provocatively tries to carve out a different sort of space for the beautiful, ideally out of the reaches of such purposive investments in its being. He clearly states that:

Taste is the faculty of estimating an object or a mode of representation by
means of a delight or aversion *apart from any interest.* The object of such a
delight is called *beautiful.*

(Kant 1988a, §5)

The beautiful is radically unlike the agreeable and unlike the good. It is 'the one and only *disinterested* and *free* delight' (Kant 1988a, §5; *my italics*). Indeed, for Kant beauty creates a space for freedom:

All interest presupposes a want or calls one forth; and being a ground
determining approval, deprives the judgement of the object of its freedom.

(Kant 1988a, §5)

What is intriguing about Kant's proposition is that we are being asked to think of 'freedom' in terms that are not directly political or ethical. So how does this 'freedom' express itself? Or, to use deliberately instrumentalising terms – the very terms Kant tells us not to employ when discussing the beautiful – how would this freedom 'cash out' in our society? Kant suggests that the beautiful 'cultivates a certain liberality of thought', which certainly does not mean that he equates freedom with the supposed choices that neo-liberalism presents to us as consumers (Kant 1988a, §29, 'General Remark ... ').

How can beauty solicit us to think beyond what is already on offer to us and how can architecture make a contribution to creating what will be defined as the 'utopian project' of aesthetic judgement?

We will have to keep returning to this important question of how architectural beauty can relate to political and social alternatives, to as-yet-unknown freedoms, even if, or rather, *especially as*, there is not necessarily a clear-cut answer to be easily found.

We must remark upon Kant's unusual use of the term 'disinterest' (Kant 1988a, §5). It sounds so turned-off, apathetic, so 'couldn't care less', so lacking in liveliness, disengaged, indifferent, indeed joyless. These impressions might well be reinforced by Kant's differentiation between the beautiful and the agreeable (which would include those human comforts that makes us happy). Nevertheless, over and over again Kant associates this 'disinterested' aesthetic appreciation with a positive and invigorating 'feeling of life':

> To apprehend a regular and appropriate building with one's cognitive faculties, be the mode of representation clear or confused, is quite a different thing from being conscious of this representation with an

accompanying sensation of delight. Here the presentation is referred wholly to the Subject, and what is more to its feeling of life [*das Lebensgefühl* (*des Subjekts*)].

(Kant, 1988a, §1)

Our 'disinterested' pleasure in a building's beauty has nothing to do with our conceptualised appreciation of its appearance, or with the hows and whys of its construction.

<u>We appreciate a building's beauty, or what strikes 'us' as beautiful, as living beings whose sense of being alive is intensified and heightened by this encounter.</u>

The subject in question catches a glimpse of the 'absolute worth' of existence as a 'person' and is thereby potentially transformed, as we will see (Kant 1988a, §4). Ruskin and Morris also feel strongly about human worth and its relation to the aesthetic. However, in contrast to Kant, beauty for them can be associated both with the agreeable and the good. Kant feels the need to defend beauty's autonomy against these 'interests'. We need to understand why.

As we have already indicated, important to Kant's analysis of the 'purely' beautiful is its freedom, autonomy, non-instrumentality. Our understanding of what a building like La Fondation Louis Vuitton signifies, in Kantian terms, would be dependent, not so much on the intention that lies behind it, but more on how we receive and appreciate 'it', and also what relations 'it' prompts us to create between ourselves. Indeed, ultimately the beautiful is not necessarily identifiable with a specific object, it does not owe its existence to some-thing. When 'it' comes to beauty, something happens in and to us in a representational realm that is independent of an 'objective reality'. Kant purports that in matters of taste:

[All] one wants to know is whether the mere representation of the object is to my liking, no matter how *indifferent* I may be to the real existence of the object of this representation. It is quite plain that in order to say that the object is beautiful and to show that I have taste, everything turns on the meaning which I can give to this representation, and not on any factor which makes me dependent on the real existence of the object. Everyone must allow that a judgement on the beautiful which is tinged with the slightest *interest*, is very partial and not a pure judgement of taste. One must not be in the least prepossessed in favour of the real existence of the thing, but must preserve complete *indifference* in this respect, in order to play the part of judge in matters of taste.

(Kant 1988a; §2 *my italics*)

For Kant, something like La Fondation Louis Vuitton ultimately does not really matter: it doesn't really have to exist at all for us, or it could disappear tomorrow and that would not necessarily be a great loss in itself. What counts for Kant is what happens between us, as people susceptible to beauty, and capable of sharing the powerful feelings of the 'furtherance of life' it can provoke within and between us (Kant 1988a, §23). However, the shared appreciation it can engender is far from being guaranteed. It cannot be manufactured, only conditions for its eventual possibility can be facilitated. These moments are often rare;

beauty reveals itself sporadically and unexpectedly. It arrives like a gift.

The beautiful is a gift [*un don*]. Drawing on the work of Marcel Mauss (1985) and Lewis Hyde (2006), we can assert that gifts are definitely different from commodities, and are even to be distinguished from presents. In his account of the realisation of the 'utopian' project of La Fondation Louis Vuitton, Jean-Paul Claverie, Arnault's adviser, declares that it is:

the present [*le cadeau*] of a patron who has expressed all his passion for creation and for art, and a business manager who has mobilised human talents and material means so as to offer a supplement of soul to his contemporaries.

(*Connaissances des arts* 2014b, 11)

'Presents' are meant to be fit for a particular purpose. They intend to be appropriate for a specific occasion, such as a birthday. They can also be a means by which one acknowledges an act of generosity, such as an invitation to someone's house for an evening meal. One buys, or can possibly craft, a present with an intention in mind. A 'successful' present would be one whose recipient recognises and appreciates the intention motivating it. This recognition and appreciation is what is interesting in the present. By contrast, Kant has made it clear that when we judge something to be beautiful, we are 'dis-interested'. We are not completely ourselves, but are another sort of person. We have relinquished our habitual 'aims and objectives'. When we judge something to be beautiful, we have entered into a quite different mental, but also, quite probably, physical space. 'There' we possibly encounter not only others, but also ourselves with them, differently. Kant points out that we would not say:

> this object (the building we are looking at, the garment that man is wearing, the concert we are listening to, the poem put up to be judged) is beautiful *for me*.
>
> (Kant 1988a, §7)

The beautiful is not about us and what we like: 'no-one cares about that' states Kant bluntly. We have projected ourselves beyond our own personal likes and dislikes and have situated ourselves at a different, higher level. Kant explains:

> if [one] proclaims something to be beautiful, then [one] requires the same liking from others; [one] judges not just for [oneself] but for everyone and speaks of beauty *as if* it were a property of things.
>
> (Kant 1988a, §7; *my italics*).

Beauty is not an intrinsic property of a thing that could be objectively verified. However, we speak of it *as if it were*. When we declare that a building is beautiful, we are presenting what is ultimately a subjective judgement, but, as we have seen, not one which is motivated by any ulterior interest, and one that is more than a mere 'personal feeling' (Kant 1988a, §29). By contrast, if we say not 'this house is beautiful' but 'this house is comfortable', we are talking about an agreeable, homely sense that we experience when we occupy its space (Kant 1988a, §8). For Kant, we are no longer talking about a judgement of taste. The example that Kant himself uses is the rose:

> the agreeableness of the rose's smell ... gives no claim to [the delight of every one]: its smell delights one person, it makes another dizzy.
>
> (Kant 1988a, §32)

The other person cannot do anything about their personal response to the rose's smell; their dislike is a gut reaction. Nor can I. I just love the perfume. We will just have to beg to differ on the issue experienced at this level of what is agreeable or not to us. When it comes down to it, our difference of opinion is not that important. However, when we say 'this rose is beautiful', we are in principle soliciting and expecting a corroborative response from those who could be with us. It is as if we were always saying 'this rose is beautiful, *isn't it*' or 'objectively speaking, as it were, I consider this rose to be a beautiful specimen, *don't you*?'. Ideally I am not asking whether someone personally likes the rose or not, and I myself am not just expressing a personal opinion. We are openly appealing to others in a different register. We concurrently expose ourselves to their disagreement, with no conclusive means of persuading them to see eye-to-eye with us and to join us – a transformed 'us' – on a higher plane. It would mean something for us to encounter each other at this level, in this other, alternative 'space' removed from our usual vested interests. Beauty might be in the eye of the beholder, inasmuch as it is not an intrinsic property of things, but something that we as subjects ascribe to the objects around us. Nevertheless, even if we know that some might find the rose or building beautiful and others not, we boldly venture to claim 'universal validity' for our aesthetic judgement. We take the risk of presenting what is ultimately a subjective judgement about the rose, or building, as a judgement which could be universally agreed with, *as if* it were an objective quality. Kant makes clear the boldness of this gesture in the following lines:

> A judgment of taste determines its object in respect of our liking (beauty) [but] makes a claim to everyone's assent, *as if* it were an objective judgment.
>
> (Kant 1988a, §32)

Our 'claim' on others' agreement is ultimately groundless. We do not have a leg to stand on. We have nothing to base our judgement on; for instance, we have no inside information or knowledge about the rose or building that could strengthen our case. We have not dissected the rose (like a botanist) or analysed the structure of the building (like a structural engineer) to extract its essential beauty. In any case, we would not find 'it': beauty is not an intrinsic property of a thing, Kant has already clearly told us that. Indeed, even the botanist when he finds a rose beautiful is speaking like 'a primitive, without culture', to quote Barthes (1984, 7) when he talks about photography.

> **Flowers are free beauties of nature. Hardly any one but a botanist knows the true nature of a flower, and even he, while recognising in the flower the reproductive organ of the plant, pays no attention to this natural end when using his taste to judge of its beauty.**
>
> (Kant 1988a, §16)

The botanist knows all there is to know about flowers. Nevertheless, when he utters 'that rose is beautiful (isn't it)?', he is no longer analysing a fine specimen of a reproductive organ, well-designed to serve its natural purpose. Beauty has nothing to do with what something is supposed to be. Beauty does not permit us to know an object any better. Kant is quite categorical about how 'useless' beauty is for understanding anything:

> an aesthetic judgment is quite unique, and affords absolutely no, (not even a confused,) knowledge of the Object.
>
> (Kant 1988a, §15)

Hence, when the botanist expresses his appreciation of a rose's beauty, he is no longer speaking from the standpoint of his professionalised self. He has instead moved to a different space where specialisms do not have a bearing. In this more inclusive space, we could also join him as his equal.

<u>The judgement and the gesture towards the other in the implied 'isn't it' of aesthetic judgement is therefore a generous gesture towards others; it creates social links. It opens up possibilities and is thereby experimental</u>

(Kant's term is 'reflective', as compared with 'determinant') (Kant, 1988a, Introduction IV; these terms will be explained later). While beauty has at all costs to resist being used as a means to an end, it could eventually 'serve' to transform ourselves and others around us.

The judgement of taste is not 'egoistic'. We break away from our conventionally materialistic ways of thinking about the world around us. We interrupt the drive to appropriate things that is probably a symptom of our defensive siege mentality, which defines others either as our property or as enemies who are out to dispossess us. We are not interested in what we can 'get' from looking at something beautiful. Aesthetic judgement takes us beyond the confines of the individualistic self as it 'must necessarily, from its inner nature, be allowed a "pluralistic validity" ' (Kant 1988a, §29). This 'pluralistic validity' means that the aesthetic judgement entails a community of persons, that could be partly in existence, could remain virtual, or that could be yet to come. Indeed,

<u>with aesthetic judgement we are attempting to build a bridge</u> <u>between our more-than subjective experience of the encounter</u> <u>with the beautiful while hopefully anticipating the receptivity of</u> <u>others (physically or potentially 'there').</u>

Kant proposes that taste is a 'kind of *sensus communis*'. By so doing he shakes up our usual understanding of the term. 'Common sense' is normally understood as a form of basic knowledge that is simply, or even banally, 'there', in this world, close to hand, within reach of everyone were they to put their minds to it. Kant in effect provocatively redefines the everyday phrase 'just use your common sense' in the same way, as we saw earlier, he did with the term 'disinterest':

> [*Sensus communis* (common sense) is] a critical faculty which in its reflective act takes account (*a priori*) of the mode of representation of everyone else, in order, *as it were*, to weigh its judgment with the collective reason of mankind, and thereby avoid the illusion arising from subjective and personal conditions which could readily be taken for objective, an illusion that would exert a prejudicial influence upon its judgment. This is accomplished by weighing the judgment, not so much with actual, as rather with the merely possible, judgment of others, and by putting ourselves in the position of everyone else, as a result of a mere abstraction from the limitations which contingently affect our own estimate.
>
> (Kant 1988a, §40)

Rather than being something that we can reliably fall back on, 'common sense' here is a projection of something that probably does not (yet) exist, but that could maybe (in the future). We seem to enter another sort of space that is less *actually*, and more *virtually*, 'there'. The capacity of being able to overcome one's individualistic limitations [*Schranken*] and put oneself 'in the position of everyone else' would be a marvellous transformation of the self. Our potential entry into this 'utopian' space does not mark a leaving-behind of differences of opinion, or even passionate dispute, in the name of some rather bland consensus. Far from it. As we already know, in a 'disinterested' way we wish to engage with others about some 'thing' that enlivens us. We appeal to them with our explicit or implicit 'isn't?' for approbation of our assertion that 'this is beautiful'. This ultimately unjustifiable conviction is nevertheless proposed by us as being valid for everyone else, or at least we passionately solicit the agreement of others. We are 'suitors for the agreement of everyone else, because we [feel] fortified with a ground, common to all' (Kant 1988a, §19). We *venture* to propose our aesthetic judgement as being universally valid. Indeed, the aesthetic judgement *is* an *adventure* which boldly proposes to 'move' from the realm of the subjective to that of the universal with little to guide us (as our 'reflective' judgement is not governed by concepts or determined by principles). To enter this lively world where the 'collective reason of mankind' is at play would be what we might call a 'sublime' experience. Kant suggests that the beautiful, in its own way, gives us a glimpse of this prospect. (We examine Kant's notion of the sublime in Chapter 4.)

If we are on the receiving end of someone's aesthetic judgement, we might well object to their implied assumption that we should agree with them, that we are somehow 'wrong' if we do not find something to be as beautiful as they apparently do. We might therefore take advantage of their exposure to dissent in the 'isn't it?'. Hence an aesthetic judgement can lead to animated debate as, Kant makes clear, each person is autonomous in this exchange and cannot be persuaded or intimidated into agreement:

> **Taste lays claim simply to autonomy. To make the judgement of others the determining ground of one's own would be heteronomy.**
>
> **(Kant 1988a, §32)**

However knowledgeable the other person is, for example, about architectural history, they cannot provide us with indubitable proof that we are wrong in our 'failure' to see beauty. Their informed insistence about aesthetic value might possibly lead us to reconsider our standpoint, visit more buildings, read more books, go to more exhibitions, in an attempt to cultivate our taste, but ultimately we pass our aesthetic judgements freely, as autonomous beings. Culture can give us a context for our aesthetic judgement, but no proof. We cannot apply aesthetic principles established by notable critics so as to determine in our own minds what is beautiful or not. We might get to understand more why others have found, for example, Chartres Cathedral to be a beautiful work of art, but if it doesn't 'do it' for us, no amount of cultivation of taste, no authoritative guidelines by supposed 'experts' will help. It is exactly this lack of guideline that makes aesthetic judgement so creative as, by itself, it *reflects* on a particular natural phenomenon, or a particular cultural artefact. It hunts around for ways of understanding it, or of relating to it, of making sense of the response it provokes in us, rather than applying ready-made principles in a *determinant* way onto the particular object. Determinant judgement has a tool box ready to apply to the particular things it encounters; reflective judgement is largely unprepared for the encounter with the particular artefact (Kant 1988a, Introduction IV). It is pleasantly taken by surprise in this way, and it therefore has to find ways of responding by itself. It is this activity that is valorising for the human as she or he is keenly experiencing her/his autonomy, freedom, capacity for growth and self-overcoming.

The passing of aesthetic judgement about the beautiful has been presented, not only as a bold adventure, but also as a risky and vulnerable 'gesture' or 'move'. Grappling with this contradiction will permit us to deepen our analysis of aesthetic value in architecture. As we know already, Kant differentiated between the beautiful and what is agreeable (and what is good). Hence, when he tells us that 'to estimate beautiful objects as such what is required is taste', he does not mean what is 'tasty', i.e. what appeals to the taste buds or what generally titillates the senses. Indeed, any sensationalising 'hype' is in principle proscribed as a 'barbaric' addition to the beautiful object:

> Taste that requires an added element of charm and emotion for its delight not to speak of adopting this as the measure of its approval, has not yet emerged from barbarism.
>
> (Kant 1988a, §13)

Here, Kant is wanting to distinguish between a 'pure' beauty, that can somehow stand for itself, from what needs added ingredients to advertise its attractions and to pull in the punters. Likewise, he disassociates the tasteful person from those whose interest in beauty stems from the art market, with its fashions, celebrities and fans:

> If man with taste enough to judge of works of fine art with the greatest correctness and refinement readily leaves the room in which he meets with those beauties that minister to vanity, or at least, social joys, and betakes himself to the beautiful in nature, so that he may there find as if were a feast of his soul in a train of thought which he can never completely evolve, we will regard this his choice with veneration, and give him credit for a beautiful soul, to which no connoisseur or art collector can lay claim on the score of the interest which his objects have for him.
>
> (Kant 1988a, §42)

Earlier on, we discussed beauty as something that arrives unexpectedly, like a visitation. True to its ungraspable nature, here too in this passage,

beauty is seen to inspire a 'train of thoughts' that cannot be wholly appropriated by the mind (as an idea or concept), let alone possessed as a commodity that has been sold and bought.

Kant obliges us to consider art's relation to the commercial world. To return to our test-case example of La Fondation Louis Vuitton: we would have to consider to what extent the building, and the artworks along with it, have been branded and packaged by the group LVMH. Is our relation to this project permeated by mediation, or can we still 'get at' it with 'our own eyes'? For Kant, a direct relation with the beautiful is all-important for the autonomy of taste. He writes:

> Whether a dress, a house or a flower is beautiful is a matter upon which one declines to allow one's judgement to be swayed by any reasons or principles. We want to get a look at the Object with own eyes, just as if our delight depended on sensation.
>
> (Kant 1988a, §8)

Today our world is dominated by visual culture and publicity. As we discussed earlier, this social phenomenon had already been evoked by Lefebvre back in the 1970s. Nowadays it is even more 'challenging' (to use the managerial euphemism), if not already impossible, to maintain the fresh, independent immediacy that Kant requires of us.

In contemporary society, visual 'charms' [*Reize*] are used in an aggravated (intensified) way. One might add, with aggravating effects. As the German language itself suggests, the agreeableness of charm taken too far can lead to a disagreeable irritation [*Reizung*], which is annoying or tiresome. Today's tendency to heighten the visual appeal of buildings is seriously put to the test by Kant's proposal that the design of form is the essential ingredient of the aesthetic taste for beauty. Kant states that:

> In painting, sculpture, and in fact in all the visual arts, including architecture and horticulture, so far as fine arts, design is what is essential. Here it is not what gratifies in sensation but merely what pleases by its *form*, that is the fundamental prerequisite for taste.
>
> (Kant 1988a, §14)

Kant advocates that a uniform 'purity', which is 'undisturbed, uninterrupted by any alien sensation', is a prerequisite for the appreciation of form. One might consider that today such a calm purity is increasingly disrupted by the bedazzling colorisation of building façades. There is a place for colour in architecture in Kant's world, as is evident in the following passage:

> The colours which illuminate the outline are part of the charm. They may no doubt, in their own way, enliven the object for sensation, but make it really worth looking at and beautiful they cannot.
>
> (Kant 1988a, §14)

However, it could be argued that today's fashionable colorisation of numerous buildings often serves to obfuscate the shape of buildings and to heighten the illusion of their movement. We lose sight of whether something is 'really worth looking at' as our senses are at least initially agreeably stimulated to the detriment of any capacity for judgement. This stylish development is an aspect of the wider trend to 'pixelate' and 'wallpaperise' architecture, made possible by digital technology (see, e.g. Picon 2013, 29).

Following Leonhard Euler (evoked earlier in relation to Königsberg's seven bridges), Kant is prepared to accept that colours are 'vibrations (*pulsus*) of the ether in uniform temporal sequence'. He can also believe that:

> the mind perceives *not only, by sense*, the effect that these vibrations have on the excitement of the organ, *but also, by reflection*, the regular play of the impressions (and hence the form in the connection of different presentations).
>
> (Kant 1988a, §14)

He is therefore far from discounting colour as producing merely pathological sensations that we should guard ourselves from. If they are 'simple', colours can be constitutive of form. They can even be part of the forming process. They can shape form. They can be: 'the formal determination of the unity of manifold of these [sensations]'. In which case colours can 'even by themselves be considered beauties'. When colour consolidates form, it does not merely appeal to sensation, but it also invigorates our reflection of beauty. The added interest of colour can stimulate what might otherwise be a rather 'dry liking' of an object. However, colour cannot 'heighten' beauty with its charms. Such a forcing, or artificial boosting, of beauty signals that charms have been taken too far; they are no longer tasteful, indeed they are symptoms of 'crude and uncultivated taste' (Kant 1988a, §14). They are a sign of a weakness and not an expression of strength.

Our urban environment features more and more colour, intended to boost the vitality or soften the hard edges of our living and working spaces. For instance, it could be considered that one such intervention, Urban Splash's recent revamp of the 'Brutalist' Park Hill estate in Sheffield (architects: Jack Lynn, Ivor Smith and John Lewis Womersley 1957–1961), detracts from the very nature of the original architectural style. Reyner Banham characterised 'Brutalism' as: 'the clear exhibition of structure, the valuation of materials "as found" and the memorability as image' (Banham cited in Chadwick 2016, 39). Arguably, these strong features are all diluted by the fashionably colourful make-over. More generally,

<u>colorisation runs the risk of becoming a formatted recipe for</u>

<u>rendering ultimately banal spaces superficially interesting,</u>

<u>stirring up our emotions and giving us a semblance of a world</u>

<u>that is on the move, where to we do not quite know …</u>

Although we might not be convinced by Kant's confident conclusiveness, it is important to at least attempt to ask how far one can go down this route before something becomes, in his terms, 'distasteful'.

As we have seen, Kant attempts to distinguish between those qualities and degrees of 'charms' that can attend, and even be part of beauty, and those

Sauerbruch & Hutton's colourful Jessop West Building, University of Sheffield 2008.

that are 'foreign' to, and even parasitic on it. In order to belong to the world of aesthetic taste, he suggested that colour should contribute to making form 'more clearly, definitely and completely intuitable' (not less) and to 'excit[ing] and sustain[ing] the attention directed to the object itself' (Kant 1988a, §14). Colour should not draw too much attention to itself otherwise, instead of reinforcing form, it undermines it. At this point of his analysis, Kant quite logically moves onto a wider discussion of 'ornament' and what is 'proper' to it. However, here too we not only appreciate the issues he obliges us to address, but will also probably be left not quite convinced by his conclusions. The very idea of ornament having clear-cut 'properties' might strike us as misguided, but we will nevertheless follow his line of thought and return later to the issue of the colourful 'wallpaperisation' of much contemporary architecture.

For Kant, 'ornament' [*Zierarten* or *parerga*] is an 'adjunct' [*Zutat*], i.e. it does not belong as an 'intrinsic constituent in the complete representation of the object'.

His examples are 'frames of pictures or the drapery on statues, or the colonnades of palaces' (Kant 1988a, §14). Ornament is to be distinguished from 'finery' [*Schmuck*]. 'Finery' is an addition that goes too far and as a consequence mars 'genuine beauty'. Kant offers the following explanation:

> if the ornament does not itself consist in the beautiful form – if it is imported like a gold frame merely to win approval for the picture by means of its charm it is then called finery and takes away from the genuine beauty.
> (Kant 1988a, §14)

However, it is difficult to know when ornament starts developing a life of its own that undermines 'beautiful form', rather than consolidating it. Indeed, picture frames, draperies on statues and colonnades on buildings could be deemed to be excessive, over-the-top. They conspicuously draw attention to themselves with their particular charms. When, at what point, could one ever definitely say that the ornament is 'in' the 'beautiful form', rather than tacked on, or tagging along? How can some things rather paradoxically *belong* in some way *as an addition* and others (of the same type) be categorised as parasitically alien? Caryatids – figures, often mythological, that are used as columns to support an entablature – provide one of the clearest instances of the dilemma with which Kant's analysis confronts us as to what 'properly' belongs to architecture and what not. Are caryatids simply sculptures, i.e. are they evidently different from architecture? Sculpture is characterised by Kant as:

> [the] art that exhibits concepts of things corporeally as they might exist in nature (though as a fine art, it does so with a concern for aesthetic purposiveness).
> (Kant 1988a, §51)

Kant restricts sculpture, albeit in a rather paradoxical way, to representing things *as they could exist* in nature. This potential verisimilitude whereby sculptures can '*almost* [be] confused with nature' means that this art form often has recourse to allegory to convey its 'aesthetic ideas', especially if they relate to such disagreeable – Kant's term is 'disgusting' – subjects such as death and war (Kant 1988a, §48). Kant concludes that 'thus statues of human beings, gods, animals, and so on belong to sculpture' (Kant 1988a, §51). Does this analysis help us to place caryatids definitively? Or are we left toying with the question:

are caryatids not just sculptures, but also, in some way, an integral part of architecture?

However, here we encounter a problem. Kant draws a clear distinction between sculpture and architecture. Having just given what are for him clear examples of sculptures, he then proceeds to roll out the following examples of architecture:

> on the other hand, temples, magnificent buildings for public gathering or again residences, triumphal arches, columns, cenotaphs and so on, erected as honorary memorials, belong to architecture.

His reasoning, by now familiar to us, is that:

> In architecture the main concern is what *use* is to be made of the artistic object, and this use is a condition to which the aesthetic ideas are confined.
>
> (Kant 1988a, §51)

We have already postulated that architecture's 'use' does not necessarily have to be perceived negatively as a drag on its aesthetic freedom. The '[architectural] product's adequacy for a certain use' might be what bestows upon this art form its specificity.

Architecture might have to negotiate more societal issues than other art forms, while still having to make a bid for its aesthetic autonomy.

Caryatids, rue des petites écuries, Paris 10e.

In any case, the term 'use' also requires refining. As mentioned earlier, 'use' might just mean that the building is expected to stand up for a certain, maybe quite minimal, amount of time. Or, being unbuildable as it 'stands', a project's 'use' might be to feature as a laboratory of ideas for the future. Far from being necessarily restrictive, Kant's association of architecture with 'use' unwittingly opens up many interesting questions about architecture's destination. The same applies to his attempt to detach architecture from nature, again in contrast to sculpture (whose products are *almost* natural). He asserts that:

> Architecture is the art of exhibiting concepts of things that are possible *only through art*, things whose form does not have nature as its determining basis but instead has a chosen purpose, and of doing so in order to carry out that intention and yet also with aesthetic purposiveness.
>
> (Kant 1988a, §51)

Again we have to object. Kant ties architecture too tightly to the architect's intention to serve a purpose when, at least structural engineers, if not architects, know that 'nature' and its laws underpin all projects that aim to stand their ground. Indeed, working in parallel with natural forms, exploring the creative affinities that can exist between architecture and nature, can produce the most ethereal and dream-like of creations, which are nevertheless, or even precisely for that reason, highly performative, as evidenced by the lightweight structures of the recently deceased Frei Otto. Otto set out to explore the 'mysterious concordances between nature and technics', thereby following in the wake of D'Arcy Thompson, who wrote:

> The search for differences or fundamental contrasts between the phenomena of organic and inorganic, of animate and inanimate things, has occupied many men's minds, while the search for community of principles or essential similarities has been pursued by few.
>
> (Thompson 1961, 7; also cited in Otto 1982, 6)

In the next chapter we will be pushing this point even further by associating Kant's (cosmo)political philosophy with the tensegral structures of Buckminster Fuller. These structures are also considered to have 'nature' as their 'determining form', and yet they can also be regarded as prime instances of highly innovative 'aesthetic ideas'.

So we have a problem with Kant's definition of architecture *per se*. For several reasons, we are also not convinced by his categorisation of caryatids as clear instances of sculpture (and not architecture). Caryatids could easily be considered to be 'useful' supplements of the building's 'beautiful form'. They lend emphatic gravity to the entrance. They symbolically reinforce the threshold which not only marks, but also creates, the difference between the outside and the inside of the property. The mythological figures also feature as protective overseers of the household, ideally establishing the inhabitants as people of a certain social standing. While being carriers of all these aesthetic ideas and social realities, caryatids might also even carry out essential structural support to the edifice (by holding a balcony).

This unavoidable confusion between sculpture and architecture becomes even more flagrant when it comes to the Baroque style. Here, the sculptural figures seem to grow out of the walls; they are part of the same organism, not tacked-on extras. As the art historian, Heinrich Wölfflin (1864–1945), vividly described:

> The baroque neutralises line as a boundary, it multiplies edges, and while the form in itself grows intricate and the order more involved, it becomes increasingly difficult for the individual parts to assert their validity as plastic values; a (purely) visual movement is set going over the sum of the forms, independently of the particular viewpoint. *The wall vibrates, the space quivers in every corner.*
>
> (Wölfflin 1950, 65; *my italics*)

With the Baroque, the walls themselves burgeon into varied sculptural forms that push at the frontiers of more classical taste. By so doing, it mimics the 'luxuriant variety' of untamed nature itself that provides 'constant food' for our aesthetic taste, whereas imposed staid 'regularity' on the natural just ends up becoming 'an irksome restraint' to our imaginations (Kant 1988a, §22). Indeed the Baroque style poses us with a question of what is happening: 'Is the artificial becoming naturalised, or is the natural becoming artificialised?' (Hocquenghem and Schérer 2013, 191). It is difficult, if not impossible, to draw clear-cut distinctions between architecture and sculpture, the natural (essential) and the artificial (additional). There is what Jacques Derrida has called a 'supplementary' relation between the two, whereby the exact location of limits, and hence of the point of their transgression, flounders (Derrida 1986, 144).

We have established that Kant wants to differentiate between 'ornament' and 'finery'. Earlier, we charted his analogous attempt to distinguish between charms which support, and those that undermine, beauty. We also examined his proposal that architecture in any case is weighed down by 'purpose' and, as a consequence, any beauties it produces are merely 'adherent'. Let us now reconsider his examples of ornamental 'self-subsiding' or 'free' beauties, particularly those that could relate to architecture, namely 'designs *à la grecque*, the foliage on borders or on wallpapers' (Kant 1988a, §16), in the light of our previous analysis of 'wallpaperisation', whether coloured or not, of

Santa Maria della Pietà, via Torremuzza, Palermo.

buildings (Picon 2013, 29). Earlier we saw that Kant defined 'free beauty' as what pleases by its own accord, independent of any purpose or concept that would otherwise have to be served. As examples thereof he listed: 'flowers, parrots, humming-birds, birds of paradise and a lot of crustaceans in the sea ... designs *à la grecque*, the foliage on borders or on wallpapers ... fantasias in music' (Kant 1988a, §16). Building on our already established faltering sense of the stability of Kant's terms, we can now ask: when do the decorative motifs found increasingly on contemporary buildings 'please freely and on their account' as they 'have no intrinsic meaning; they represent nothing – no Object under a definite meaning'? And when are they signs of trendy 'wallpaperisation', whereby the charming 'finery' just drapes (i.e. adds itself to) what could be a banal structure, but maybe precisely by so doing fulfils its intention: the production of a spectacular, albeit superficial, appeal? Such an 'appeal' could be applied as a make-over to any sort of building, regardless of its function. Charming ornament thereby becomes a type of camouflage, which in effect provides an anonymous screen for any type of enterprise. This recent development in architectural practice could be seen as eroding Kant's oft-repeated statement that architecture can necessarily only produce 'appendant beauty' as buildings are predetermined by 'what the thing has to be' (Kant 1988a, §16). For example, I would suggest that Francis Soler's Ministry of Culture, with its conspicuous exploitation of ornament, could be anything. As Picon also points out in reference to this building, 'computer software makes possible the texturing of *any* surface with *any* picture' regardless of a building's use (Picon 2013, 29). We might therefore think that such an edifice boldly resists Kant's attempt to relegate architecture to what could be conceived as a subordinate place. It could be seen as fulfilling, against his design, the requirement for 'pure beauty' to produce a 'delight' that 'rests immediately upon the way the figure strikes the eye', independent of any consideration of its 'serviceability' for a predetermined 'purpose' (Kant 1988a, General Remark). Or, by contrast, we might think that such a building loses sight of what is so different and challenging about architecture (compared to other art forms), namely its oscillation between 'spectacle and use' (see Vidler 2008).

What is (maybe) so different and challenging about architecture (compared to other art forms) is its oscillation between 'spectacle and use'.

We would also have to consider what sort of space it invites us to enter if we do indeed find it beautiful. Drawing on the 'utopian' impetus of Kant's *Critique of Judgement*, we should ask whether, thanks to the occasion a building

Francis Solers' French Ministry of Culture, Paris 2004: an instance of 'wallpaperisation'.

can produce, we can encounter ourselves and each other differently when exchanging our reactions to the 'universal[ising]' proposition 'this building is beautiful, *isn't it?*'. If pure aesthetic judgement necessitates us leaving behind our instrumentalising mindset (all too complicit with the economic forces prevalent in contemporary capitalist society), what leverage for implicit critique does this project, for instance, propose, if any? This is a difficult question to respond to, but it is one that Kant could be seen as posing to us each time we experience architectural works.

Kant is categorically against the artificial manipulation of beauty. For him it provokes 'displeasure' or even 'disgust' (Kant 1988a, §22, General Remark, §48; see Derrida 1975, 87–93). For instance, Kant would probably find it inconceivable that cosmetic surgery, which artificially forces nature into a pleasing form and passes off the transfiguration as 'natural', could be thought to produce the beautiful. However, one might understand why people resort to correcting their appearance when Kant, employing a highly classicist and prejudicial vocabulary, tells us that beauty presupposes a certain harmony, symmetry, regularity, and that any 'perversity of form', such as that displayed by 'one eyed animals', is fundamentally displeasing (Kant 1988a, §22). However, Kant would be uncompromising on this score. Cosmetic surgery is a form of trickery akin to that often played on those city-types who are eager to experience Nature. Kant describes a scenario whereby their 'jovial' country host, wanting to 'sell' them the full excursion package, adds the attractive feature of the nightingale's song. Given that the bird cannot be relied upon to deliver on command, he employs a local lad who can simulate its musical beauty with reeds. At first the city-folk are enchanted, then, on discovering the 'fraud' practised on them, they are more than disappointed, they are outraged and disgusted. The same goes for the exposure of other forms of mischievous, or equally, of commercially interested, machinations such as the planting of 'artificial flowers' and the perching of 'artfully carved birds' to swell the impression of natural beauty (Kant 1988a, §42). However, we have already seen how problematic the attempt is to redeem 'genuine beauty' from what is deemed to be a completely artificial addition. Kant's difficulty is hardly surprising, given his understandable refutation of the notion that beauty could ever be an essential property of a thing that could be clearly identified, protected and thereby conserved.

Beauty that is used to achieve social success – such as is the case with 'celebrities' – would be disgusting for Kant. Here, 'finery' is used to impress 'the eyes of others' so as to nourish the interests of vanity (Kant 1988a, §42). As we have seen, 'pure beauty' is also not to be artificially reproduced, neither is it to be produced formulaically, by rote as it were, according to some preset model or prototype (Kant 1988a, §17). Indeed it resists all forms of forcing, hence the difference between poetry and rhetoric. Whereas the latter can be employed as part of a manipulative and deceptive 'machinery of persuasion', the former innocently 'plays with semblance' and as such is the perfect medium for aesthetic ideas (Kant 1988a, §53).

Kant describes the beauty of poetry as follows:

> Poetry (which owes its origin almost entirely to genius and is least willing to be led by percepts or example) holds the first rank among all the arts. It expands the mind by giving freedom to the imagination and by offering,

from among the boundless multiplicity of possible forms accordant with a given concept, to whose bounds it is restricted, that one which couples with the presentation of the concept a wealth of thought to which no verbal expression is completely adequate, and by thus rising aesthetically to ideas.

(Kant 1988a, §53)

After poetry, it is the charms and delights of music that are best able to expand the mind's capacity to entertain stimulating aesthetic ideas even if, or even *because*, they are even more indeterminate and less graspable or communicable to others than in poems. Music can seem to transport us elsewhere, beyond our habitual limits, to a different sort of place, while soliciting our very bodies with its sound vibrations. By contrast with music, the visual arts produce more lasting impressions as their impetus is more grounded in graspable ideas. As such, Kant considers that an art form, such as painting, contributes more to the cultivation of the mind, indeed to the 'urbanity', or sophisticated refinement of the higher cognitive powers. At this point of his analysis, when comparing 'the aesthetic value of the various fine arts', Kant neglects architecture. It does not feature, at least not explicitly, and we are almost at the end of Kant's treatment of 'aesthetic judgement'. How can we implicate architecture into this analysis? Previously we were able to involve it in Kant's discussion of what belonged to the beautiful and what didn't. A disgusted rejection of an aesthetic object arose due to a, not easily determinable, 'excess' or 'forcing', sometimes indicative of commercial manipulation, that was deemed incompatible with the freedom that has to accompany the beautiful. We were able to place architecture squarely within this debate. How might architecture feature now, at this point of Kant's *Critique of Judgement*?

As a way of reintroducing architecture into the debate about what art forms constitute the best vehicles for aesthetic ideas, we might want to surreptitiously associate it with poetry. Architects can indeed write poetically about their professional activity.

The fundamentals of architecture can be conveyed in ways that not only eloquently express very down-to-earth experiences of warmth and well-being, but also conjure up a deeply spiritual sense of belongingness.

For instance, if we take some liberties with the layout of the original text, Louis Kahn writes evocative poetry when defining what, *and how*, a room is:

The room is the beginning of architecture.
You do not say the same thing in one room as you say in another,
That's how sensitive a room is.
A room is a marvellous thing,
A world within a world.
It's yours and offers a measure of yourself.
What slice of the sun enters your room?
You feel the privacy of it, you feel *that* sun belongs to you,
Coming through the window,
Playing along the sill and the jambs and the walls.
If you watch it, it belongs to you, really.
It's just your particular place,
Your particular room.

(Kahn 1991, 294)

Even the, on one level, quite banal statement, 'a room is a marvellous thing', resonates in suggestive ways once animated with a shaft of light, barely described, but pregnantly appropriated as somehow 'ours' as it contributes to the creation of a place in which we feel at home.

Equally, still in search of a place for architecture within Kant's analysis, we can demonstrate its musical qualities. It, too, can become polyphonic as Viollet-le-Duc recounts when remembering an early childhood experience in Notre Dame Cathedral. He writes as follows:

> my eyes were fixed on the stained glass rose window through which the sunbeams passed, saturated in explosive colours. I still see the place where we were immobilised by the crowd. Suddenly the immense organs made themselves heard, for me it was the rose window that I had in front of my eyes that sung. My old guide wanted to put me right, but in vain. The impression grew stronger and stronger, until I started believing that some of the panels of stained glass were producing grave tones, and others sharp tones. I was seized by so much terror, that he had to take me outside.
>
> (Viollet-le-Duc 1986, I, 22)

As John Summerson suggests: 'few writers have touched on this capacity of architecture to become "alive" with sound' (Summerson 1980, 11).

Additionally, architecture can be appreciated, not only as poetry and music, but also as one of the visual arts, given Kant's suggestion that they contribute to 'urbanity', to the refinement of social relations, rendering them more civil and courteous. Architecture is indeed supremely well-placed to promote our general education and good breeding. We again have recourse to Viollet-le-Duc, for he describes well this improving capacity of architecture when discussing Gothic cathedrals:

> [They were] not only places of worship and God's house but also the centre of intellectual activity, the depository of all the traditions of art and of all human knowledge. What we place in museums, our ancestors confided to the treasures of the church. What we look for in books, they read in living letters on doorways or in stained glass windows. This is

> why on cathedral walls we see so many of those calendars informing us about botany and zoology, about the working methods for various arts and trades, about health risks, about how best to spend one's time, about agriculture, all juxtaposed with religious scenes and moral allegories. They composed an encyclopaedia that was freely available for everyone to consult.
>
> (Viollet-le-Duc 1856, 16–17; *my translation*)

Architecture also physically provides the fabric of our towns and cities, of our urban environment. It can contribute to the enhancement of civil life. It should always remain alert to how it impacts on its environment. For Kant, such vigilance is not characteristic of music. Kant reckons that music:

> has a certain lack of urbanity about it. For it extends its influence (on the neighbourhood) farther than people wish, and so, as it were, imposes itself on others and hence impairs those outside the musical party.
>
> (Kant 1988a, §53)

Whereas the medium of music is perceived as constitutively disrespectful of limits to the extent of being a nuisance to others, an integral aspect of architecture is the consideration of its 'urbanity'. It should always take into consideration how it impresses itself on its environment. As such, it amply qualifies as a fine art that can create forms worthy of conveying 'aesthetic ideas'.

Kant concludes *Critique of Judgement* with a discussion of how the fine arts 'cultivate our mental powers by exposing ourselves beforehand to what we call *humaniora*'. For Kant, the 'humanities' signify 'both the universal feeling of sympathy' (a general feeling of participation) and the 'ability to engage universally in very intimate communication', the capacity of expressing both personal and more general thoughts (Kant 1988a, §60). Architecture can create spaces propitious to 'the art of reciprocal communication of ideas'. In certain spaces we can somehow feel mentally and physically expanded, taken out of ourselves, transported beyond our everyday preoccupations, more open to others, more willing and able to entertain novel ideas, however associative and vague. We feel the 'furtherance of life' (Kant 1988a, §23). For Kant, this would be the ultimate criteria for judging any project aesthetically, including the one that we choose as our test-case example for this chapter, La Fondation Louis Vuitton.

CHAPTER 4

From the sublime to the cosmopolitical

In the previous chapter we analysed Kant's presentation of the beautiful in *Critique of Judgement*. However, the beautiful is only one facet of his understanding of aesthetic judgement; the other is the sublime. Kant obliges us to consider how the sublime relates to the beautiful when he enigmatically suggests that there is a 'transition' from the latter to the former because of their similarities, and yet there are important differences between them which makes them quite distinct (Kant 1988a, §23). As thinkers of architecture, we are also confronted with the additional question of what repercussions his analysis of the sublime has for us, especially as we will be told that, because of its tendency towards formlessness, it ultimately cannot be captured in architectural (or indeed any other) terms (Kant 1988a, §24). These issues we will now go on to explore in detail.

The beautiful and the sublime are similar as they both please us 'for their own sake'; we are 'disinterested' when we experience them, being neither dependent on sensations of agreeableness or concepts of what is good. Our judgements of them both are also 'reflective' (moving from the particular instance facing us, towards universalising rules, principles or laws), rather than 'determinant' (whereby the particular is subsumed under pre-existing universals). We have already seen how this 'reflective' appreciation and evaluation of beauty contributes to our creative and experimental involvement with the aesthetic (Kant 1988a Intro IV). The 'risky' bridge-building exercise between what can all too easily be reduced to a subjective opinion about what is beautiful and an apparently objectively valid statement such as 'this building is beautiful' was also understood as 'utopian', inasmuch as 'we' appeal unegoistically, as sentient and finite beings momentarily distanced from ourselves and from our everyday concerns, to others. We thereby venture to assume a *sensus communis* (or 'common sense', something that we could all share), which might form the basis of a project for more egalitarian and participatory community in the future. I will be suggesting that 'utopianism' also comes into play with Kant's notion of the sublime (though differently) and that it can indirectly contribute to what we conceive of as possible and ecologically, (cosmo)politically desirable in architecture.

Having sketched out the similarities between the beautiful and the sublime, we now need to address their differences. In order to do so, we could ask ourselves why Kant discusses the sublime in the first place especially since he claims it is a 'mere appendix' to our aesthetic judgement (Kant 1988a, §23). The short answer might just be that he felt obliged to because of the lively debate stimulated by the publication of Edmund Burke's highly influential *A Philosophical Enquiry into the Origin of our Ideas of the Sublime and Beautiful* in 1757. However, over and above the historical importance of Burke's text, what other reasons can we find? What new considerations does the sublime produce for Kant's third *Critique* and, furthermore, what are their implications for architecture?

In the previous chapter we described the beautiful as soliciting an expansive gesture towards others regardless of whether it might ultimately misfire by being rebuffed, or indeed turn out to be inappropriate, as would be the case were distasteful artificiality to become apparent. The initial response to the beautiful would still remain a generous wish to share one's pleasure with others. The sublime presents us with a more complex feeling, one that is intrinsically ambivalent and contradictory and whose social implications are therefore less clear. With the sublime we have to negotiate intense factors that are working against each other, and against us. Whereas the beautiful was associated with a positive 'feeling of the furtherance of life', the sublime only provides us with an 'indirect' pleasure, one derived from an experience that is initially negative. Kant states that it is 'brought about by the feeling of momentary check [*Hemmung*] to the vital forces followed at once by a discharge [*Ergiessung*] all the more powerful' (Kant 1988a, §23). The culminative rush of energy we experience with the sublime is produced by the contrast with the immediately preceding interruption, or momentary suffocation of life. The sublime is thereby characterised by a coercive perversity that does not feature in our encounter with the beautiful.

The beautiful held out the peaceful prospect of a rich and fulfilling attunement with others, the fruition of a harmonious reconciliation between our faculties brought about by the act of appreciation. By contrast, the sublime destabilises us by confronting us abruptly with our limits, before revealing our capacity for thinking a limitless beyond.

> It presents us with something that strikes us as 'counter-purposive to our judgement, incommensurate with our capacity to represent and, as it were, violent to our imagination', before demonstrating our capacity to supersede the world of phenomena (Kant 1988a, §23). The beautiful appears to open out for us a world wherein we could naturally lead fulfilling lives were we able to overcome our conditioning 'interests'. It prepares us 'to love something, even nature, without interest' (Kant 1988a, §29). By contrast, the sublime exposes us crudely to our inadequacies and shortcomings by confronting us with disorienting scenes of 'chaos ... [and of the] wildest and most ruleless disarray and devastation' (Kant 1988a, §23). We are faced with a world that does not seem to possess any systematic unity at all and in which we are not immediately at home, before being resituated in a different relation to space.

Measuring the sublime and its relation to architecture

> Kant defines the sublime as that which is 'absolutely great', being large beyond all points of comparison (Kant 1988a, §25). We normally go about our lives assessing and categorising, often unconsciously, what is around us according to its relative situation and perceived significance. Some things loom larger in our minds than others and we tend to equate this bigness with importance, regardless of whether that size corresponds to a physical reality, or whether it is purely psychologically attributed. Sometimes we need to put things into

perspective by comparing what is apparently big with something even bigger. This act of relativisation can help us get a grip on our lives. Alternatively, as Jonathan Swift's *Gulliver's Travels* and Lewis Carroll's *Alice in Wonderland* remind us, it can open up an abysmal sense of not knowing where we stand as standards of measurement are revealed to be arbitrary, and therefore as not grounded in any sort of truthful objectivity (Swift 1982; Carroll 1992). Kant points out that these nevertheless indispensable standards are either empirically produced, or a-priori generated. In the case of the former, he tells us that we are relying on a sense of 'the average size' of, for example, 'the men known to us, of animals of a certain kind, of trees, of houses, of mountains and so forth' (Kant 1988a, §25). As Kant makes clear, the only legitimation of these standards is what is known to us through our particular experiences. Others might well have other ideas about size, having encountered different instances of things 'of a certain kind'. For example, between different cultures, and between different classes within the more or less same culture, opinions might well vary about what 'standard' accommodation is, or should be. In the case of a-priori standards, by definition we are not relying on our experiences. Nevertheless, Kant writes, 'by reason of the *deficiences* of the judging Subject' even these a-priori judgements about size are 'restricted to subjective conditions of presentation *in concreto*' (Kant 1988a, §25; *my italics*). His examples of a-priori judged standards are as follows:

> in the practical sphere, the greatness of a particular virtue, or of public liberty and justice in a country; or, in the theoretical sphere, the greatness of the accuracy or inaccuracy of an experiment or measurement, etc.
>
> (Kant 1988a, §25)

Even when considering such important abstract principles as virtue, public liberty, justice and accuracy, we have to gauge their value, and the degree of their applicability to a particular context, according to standards of measurement that could be considered inappropriate. These standards are necessarily ultimately subjective and rooted in mere concrete instances that we happen to have come across. They are therefore not on par with the idea itself. We nevertheless cannot do without them as we need somehow to add dimensions to, for example, 'freedom of speech', that we can measure in order to get some sort of tangible hold on 'it'.

Having established how comparative measurement is crucial for us as a means of evaluating our world so as to situate ourselves within a context we can have dealings with, Kant indicates what the repercussions of such relativity are. We tend to have 'respect' for what we assess to be 'large' and 'contempt' for what we consider 'small' (Kant 1988a, §25). Moreover we apply these categorisations with their corresponding affective reactions 'to anything, even to any characteristics of things'. There seems to be no way out of our 'deficient' way of sizing-up our world. We might think that any prospect for establishing a more egalitarian, less biased, 'truer' relation to the world, including with ourselves, fades even more in the following passage:

> Nothing in nature can be given, however large we may judge it, that could not, when considered in a different relation, be *degraded* all the way to the infinitely small, nor conversely anything so small that it could not, when compared with still smaller standards, be expanded for the imagination all the way to the magnitude of a world.
>
> (Kant 1988a, §25; *my italics*)

It would appear that the continuous process of relativising 'standardisation' to which we can subject everything means that nothing is immune to eventual 'degradation'. Furthermore, new technological discoveries can just exacerbate the situation: Kant cites the examples of telescopes and microscopes as tools which open up, respectively, ever larger and ever smaller worlds to our senses, thereby extending relativism way out into the universe and way into the very cells of organisms. However, as a conclusion to this section, Kant places the sublime beyond this vertiginous scaling-up and -down of the world. He writes: 'Sublime is what even to be able to think proves that the mind has a power surpassing any standard of sense.' The mind is capable of thinking the idea of totality, beyond its infinite division into parts. Whereas imagination more or less adequately attempts to synthesise fractionalised reality so as to help understanding 'progress to infinity', reason can immediately present the idea of the world as a whole. Reason can do this as it functions independently of 'objects of the senses'; its standards are therefore not finite.

In the previous chapter we were already confronted with the problem of how to situate architecture in relation to beauty. We saw that Kant ostensibly tied architecture down to purposive functionality, thereby disqualifying it as a medium for 'free beauty'. Here too, in his discussion of the sublime, we are faced with its exclusion as its very solidity would appear to be an insurmountable obstruction to something that veers toward formlessness (i.e. that cannot be contained in a delimited form). It is therefore surprising to see that Kant goes on to evoke two specific architectural examples as a way of illustrating what the sublime experience might be. The context is as follows: having established that the sublime is 'a magnitude that is equal only to itself', i.e. it is 'absolutely large', and thereby placed it outside and beyond the comparative sizing of phenomena we encounter in our world, he then continues his analysis of the 'estimation of magnitude'. He advocates that, even when accounting for size mathematically, by determining it with numbers, whatever unit of assessment or 'basic measure' [*Grundmass*] we use – his examples are 'the foot, the rod … [the] German mile or even the Earth's diameter' – we rely on an initial visualisation of what is in front of us by our intuition (Kant 1988a, §26). For Kant, intuition can strike up 'an immediate relation' to objects thanks to sensibility, which is affected by actual things, and whose representation gives us a world that we can then try to understand by means of concepts. Imagination, defined in his *Critique of Pure Reason* as 'an art concealed in the depths of the human soul', also plays a crucial role (Kant 1983, B181). The imagination can present us with objects that are otherwise absent. It can conjure up both what was there but is no longer (i.e. it can remember the past and reintroduce it into the present), and what is not here but could be (i.e. it can inject the present and the future with the possible forms of things) (Kant 1983 B181; 1974, §15). In the following passage, imagination's creative ability to remember and transform material is required to convert what we see into mathematical data (i.e. something that is not actually there). He writes:

> Hence our estimation of the magnitude of the basic measure must consist merely in our being able to take it in directly in one intuition and to use it, by means of the imagination, for exhibiting numerical concepts.
>
> (Kant 1988a, §26)

Kant suggests that, at the basis of all calculation, there is an 'aesthetic' moment. Mathematics is presented as emerging out of the initiating 'subjective', not objective, operation of the combined forces of intuition. If we cannot intuitively hold onto the 'basic measure', we will not be able subsequently to determine what is before us through calculation. Imagination keeps mathematical calculation 'alive', he says, by apprehending and comprehending what it sees, as far as it can.

At this point it would be interesting to turn to Le Corbusier's controversial notion of the Modulor as a way of measuring space and building in ways that are appropriate for us. This 'golden rule of the human scale' (based on an average height of 1.83 m) is seen by some as an inflexible principle to be imposed in every case regardless of context (Le Corbusier 1963, 116). By others, who are more attuned to his references of musical scales and harmonic modulations, the Modulor is perceived more along the lines of Poincaré's philosophy of space, a 'psychophysiological genesis of geometry' (Le Corbusier 1963, 15–17; Migayrou in Cinqualbre and Migayrou 2015, 129–134). This approach accords more importance to variation, approximation and flexibility. The Modulor would thereby respond more to Kant's suggestion that something 'imaginative' keeps calculation 'alive'.

Kant reflections on calculation could also provide us with an occasion to discuss the changes in our relation with architecture brought about by computerised calculation, which makes possible previously unrealisable forms (such as Gehry's).

<u>Where is the 'aesthetic' moment of intuition to be situated in the design-process when even modellisation is virtual?</u>

If we apply Kant's terms to this radically different context where mental arithmetic can play no role, can we decide whether computerised calculation is dead or 'alive'? We discussed earlier whether architecture was possibly a craft. Matthew Crawford's suggestion, in *The Case for Working With Your Hands*, that new technologies have brought about the material impoverishment of our world was evoked. Here we are discussing not so much the trace of the hand as the mode of functioning of the eye. To what extent do the eyes that look at the computer screen intuitively 'take in directly' or 'immediately grasp' what is before them (Kant 1988a, §26)?

Having identified the importance of the intuitively understood 'basic measure', Kant then identifies the origin of it ruination. It lies in the differences between the two operations that imagination has to combine, apprehension and comprehension. He explains that when faced with objects of a large scale:

> [a]pprehension involves no problem, for it may progress to infinity. But comprehension becomes more and more difficult the farther apprehension progresses, and it soon reaches its maximum, namely the aesthetically largest basic measure for an estimation of magnitude. For when apprehension has reached the point where the partial presentations of sensible intuition that were first apprehended are already beginning to be extinguished in the imagination, as it proceeds to apprehend further ones, the imagination then loses as much on the one side as it gains on the other; and so there is a maximum of comprehension that it cannot exceed.
>
> (Kant 1988a, §26)

It is at this point that he evokes two monuments to elucidate his point:

> This explains Savary's observations in his account of Egypt, that in order to get the full emotional effect of the size of the Pyramids we must avoid coming too near just as much as remaining too far away. For in the latter case the representation of the apprehended parts (the tiers of stones) is

but obscure, and produces no effect upon the aesthetic judgement of the Subject. In the former, however, it takes the eye some time to complete the apprehension from the base to the summit; but in this interval the first tiers always in part disappear before the imagination has taken in the last and so the comprehension is never complete. – The same explanation may also sufficiently account for the bewilderment, or sort of perplexity, which, as is said, seizes the visitor on first entering St Peter's in Rome. For here a feeling comes home to him of the inadequacy of his imagination for presenting the idea of a whole within which that imagination attains its maximum, and, in the fruitless efforts to extend this limit, recoils upon itself but in so doing succumbs to an emotional delight.

(Kant 1988a, §26)

Why does Kant use architectural examples to give us a feel for the sublime when he will insist straight afterwards that 'a pure judgement about the sublime … must have no purpose whatsoever'? We already know that he tends to tie architecture down to purposiveness. Its predetermination by 'what [it] has to be' meant that it could only furnish instances of 'appendant', not 'free', beauty (Kant 1988a, §16). He actually took a church as his example: 'Much might be added to a building that would immediately please the eye, were it not meant to be a church' (Kant 1988a, §16). In the above passage (§26) it is as if the function of St. Peter's, or indeed of the pyramids, momentarily plays no role.

The sublime is 'absolutely large'. Probably Kant thinks of architecture rather than other art forms (paintings, sculptures), as its works are generally bigger. Paintings are often bigger than us. Sculptures, such as the Statue of Liberty, can be enormous. Nevertheless, generally it is architecture that has the dimensions required to evoke the sublime. His evocation of the pyramids draws our attention to the interesting question of what the 'correct' positionality might be for appreciating a monument of that size, or indeed any building. Is there one? Too much distance reduces the pyramids to a disappointing 'blob', such was the photographer Alexander Rodchenko's experience on first seeing the Eiffel Tower

(Rodchenko 1989, 259). The same anticlimax can be felt when the site turns out to be overrun with other tourists and the whole infrastructure that they engender. There are too many competing factors that get in our way for the 'full emotional effect' of the edifice to be fully felt.

Although Kant seems to agree with Savary that being 'too close' to the pyramids is also not the right attitude to adopt, he then gives us an account of how a purportedly 'excessive' proximity creates the effects of 'inadequacy' that are part of the sublime experience. He then logically moves from pyramids (that have little interior space and were in any case not designed for easy access to their insides) to St. Peter's. This second monument combines scale with the experience of moving from outside to inside its walls. It is a peculiarity of architecture as compared with other art forms. Some sculptures can be entered. The Statue of Liberty is again a good example: one of its functions became the need to satisfy 'the public delight in climbing to a great height' (Provoyeur cited by Nye 1994, 261). Nevertheless, sculptures do not usually solicit this type of interaction, whereas it is an essential aspect of architecture. It is maybe also for this other reason that he thinks of architecture.

Kant focuses on the effects that the qualitative difference between the outside of an edifice and the gradual discovery of interior space, which can sometimes seem illogically bigger than the enveloping exterior, can provoke. Architecture can create an all-round effect that can sometimes border on the oppressive.

Despite never have left Königsberg (as we know), he has probably read travel literature about St. Peter's describing the almost overwhelming intensity of the

Close-up of pyramids. We cannot synthesise an image of the whole edifice.

emotions that the overall effect of one's entering the building can cause. His account of the vicarious experience would suggest that, contrary to Savary's analysis of the pyramids, there is no 'correct' point to be sought from which to view a building. Architecture is instead to be experienced as a *movement* or *a passage-through* its varied surfaces and immersive exposure to its different atmospheres.

An almost annihilating 'bewilderment' or 'perplexity' can be produced by entering a building, even one as classically formal as St. Peter's, when one discovers the exuberant proportions of its interior (Kant 1988a, §26). The colossal size cannot be intuitively assimilated, the imagination packs up, and yet an 'emotional delight' is perversely released as reason steps in. Asserting its superiority over sensibility and understanding, reason overcomes these other faculties' limits and 'demands totality'. Reason can think infinity as an 'immense whole'. It can think the universe or 'world edifice'. Reason's force is experienced as an act of violence by the imagination and intuition as its demands are 'counter-purposive', i.e. contrary to the way they operate. It forces a comprehension 'in one instant [of] what is [otherwise] apprehended successively' and thereby 'cancel[s] the condition of time' (Kant 1988a, §27).

Giovanni Paolo Panini 'Interior of St Peter's in Rome', 1750.

However, by means of this exposure of inadequacy, reason in effect bestows upon the imagination a nobler task; that of making itself equal to its ideas. Kant explains:

> Our imagination, even in its greatest effort to do what is demanded of it and comprehend a given object *in a whole* of intuition (and hence to exhibit an idea of reason), proves its own limitations [*Schranken*] and inadequacy, and yet at the same time proves its own vocation to [obey] a law, namely to make itself adequate to the idea.
>
> (Kant 1988a, §27)

An idea of reason, such as the infinite, whole universe broadens imagination's horizons and stimulates it to overcome its 'limitations' [*Schranken*]. We gain 'respect for our own [supersensible] vocation' (§27).

The sublime, nature and an expanded notion of architecture

Architecture is apparently left behind at this point, despite having initially almost transported us into the arms of the sublime. It would appear to have been relegated to the realm of the 'colossal', which is defined as:

> the mere exhibition of that concept if that concept is almost too large for any exhibition (i.e. if it borders on the relatively monstrous); for the *purpose* of exhibiting a concept is hampered if the intuition of the object is almost too large for our power of representation.
>
> (§27)

Here, we are straining at the limits of 'purposiveness', already identified as what is most proper to architecture as compared to other art forms. The sublime is just out of reach as it 'must have no purpose whatsoever of the object as the basis determining it' (§27). Even the scenes that wild nature can confront us with 'shapeless mountain masses piled on one another in wild disarray, with their pyramids of ice, or the gloomy raging sea' have been dropped as exemplars of the sublime. It would seem that Kant's sublime becomes a human affair. It collapses into becoming a programme for the improvement of the human species so that we can fulfil our destiny of ranking 'above nature' (§28). At most, nature features as a way for us to boost our sense of how superior to nature we ultimately are:

> Hence sublimity is contained not in any thing of nature, but only in our mind, insofar as we can become conscious of our *superiority* to nature within us and thereby also to nature outside us (as far as it influences it). Whatever arouses this feeling in us, and this includes the *might* of nature that challenges our forces, is then (although improperly) called sublime.
>
> (§28)

Faced with the 'challenges' of nature, the next obvious step could appear to be to conquer it from the 'safety' that technology provides (§28). Technology would give us the requisite distance for feeling strong like a 'warrior' and not frightened when faced by the potential dangers of nature. We acquire the 'courage' to be able to measure ourselves against the seeming omnipotence of nature' (§28). Armed with technological power, we no longer feel that our resistance to nature's might is an 'insignificant trifle', instead we feel Promethean in our capacity to instrumentalise it to achieve our aims.

But what do we actually want? Do we want to subjugate nature with our technology? In a nuclear age, do we still equate technology with safety? Also, how on earth can this combative vision of the world be reconciled in any way with the Kant we described earlier? Kant had insisted that a project for 'perpetual peace' is no vain hope but instead a goal that we should attempt to realise. Consequently he preached that it is incumbent upon us all to feel globally responsible for our actions, including those pertaining to the activity of architectural practice. We seem to have left these concerns behind with this technocratic reduction of the sublime.

An alternative reading of the sublime, one more in tune with contemporary concerns about ecology and 'cosmopolitics' (a politics that thinks of the planet as a whole), might be found by adopting a different form of architecture, if not as a model, then as a guiding or 'regulative principle'

(Kant 1983, B222). The examples Kant used, the pyramids and St. Peter's, are impressively, but also oppressively, monumental in their proportions. They are the product of a gradual accumulation and balancing of heavy stone. Back in 1940, Lewis Mumford inveighed against such monuments. He described them as a 'mass of dead buildings' that contributed to 'the immobilization of life' (Mumford 1940, 434). He proposes instead that a different way of building should be adopted. One that is lighter and more nomadic:

Why, for example, should each generation go on living in the quarters that were built by its ancestors? ... The pastoral nomad spared himself the sacrifice of the living to the dead monument until he copied the ways of men in cities: he traveled light. Civilisation today, for different reasons, with different ends in view, must follow this example of the nomad: it must not merely travel light but settle light: it must be ready, not for merely physical movement in space, but for adaptation to new conditions of life, new industrial processes, new cultural advantages. Our cities must not be monuments, but self-renewing organisms: the dominating image should not be the cemetery, where the dead must not be disturbed, but the field, meadow, and parkland, with its durable cover of trees, its light boundary lines, its changing crops for which the fields are plowed every year.

(Mumford 1940, 439–440)

Without wanting to fully endorse Mumford's provocative point of view, we might well feel that his proposition that cities, and the buildings that compose them, should be thought of as 'self-renewing organisms' is pertinent to present-day concerns about our uncoordinated relation to nature. Taking on board some of his proposals would also permit us to re-engage with those alternative ways of conceiving architecture we evoked earlier, when we critiqued Kant's conventional assumptions about what constitutes a modest 'dwelling house'. Lighter, more flexible and mobile structures were discussed, as well as troglodytes, as necessitating different modalities of building that oblige us to think differently about our relation to our environment.

It might well also be that an expanded notion of architecture would serve better justice to Kant's cosmopolitical thinking.

In his *Critique of Pure Reason*, Kant defines 'architectonics' as the 'art of constructing systems'. He presents his aim as establishing a philosophical system that is more than 'a mere aggregate of knowledge' (Kant 1983, B860).

Instead it aims to be more 'scientific'. As we saw earlier, his critical project wants to ascertain what we can, and what we cannot, know. This exercise of demarcating limits [*Grenzen*] is regarded as a necessary exercise if we are to fulfil our potential. It not only saves us time and energy, but also spares us from falling into the trap of the competing dangers of scepticism (thinking that we can know nothing), or dogmatism (thinking that we can know everything). The critical project is presented as a 'propaedeutic', or preparatory study, for putting metaphysics on this so-called 'scientific' footing. It can be conceived as a mere scaffolding, mould or formwork within which a future metaphysics will one day take shape. For his notion of the scientific, Kant calls upon biology, the study of living organisms. He accordingly describes his system in the following way with reference to Latin terms:

> The whole is thus an organised unity (*articulatio*), and not an aggregate (*coacervatio*). It may grow from within (*per intussusceptionem*) but not by external addition (*per appositionem*). It is thus like an animal body, the growth of which is not by the addition of a new member, but by the rendering of each member, without change of proportion, stronger and more effective for its purposes.
>
> (Kant 1983, B861)

Kant sees the architectonic of his system as being less 'technical' than previous ones. By this he means that it is not the product of haphazardly 'piled-up' materials, but rather the result of an organically 'articulated' [*gegleidert*] structure, akin to the growing members of a body [*Glieder*]. Held together by the 'affinities' between the component parts, the whole is animated by a germinating Idea which steadily grows in strength (Kant 1983, B862). Kant emphasises that:

> not only is each system articulated in accordance with an Idea, but they are one and all organically united in a system of human knowledge, as members of one whole [*als Glieder eines Ganzen*].
>
> (Kant 1983, B863)

The architectural metaphor employed by Kant here evidently evokes a different mode of construction from that implemented in the case of the pyramids, St. Peter's and indeed the modest 'dwelling house'. The latter was only analogous to the 'transcendental doctrine of elements'. This inventory of the basic elements of knowledge, that are not derived from experience, ascertained, for example: that space and time are a-priori forms of intuition that we cannot do without if things are to become objects of possible experience for us; and that these objects of experience are then understood by us according to the categories of quality, quantity, relation and modality. These were some of the basic building blocks he was referring to when he described his 'dwelling house' as 'just sufficiently roomy for our business on the level of experience, and just sufficiently high to allow of our overlooking it' (Kant 1983, B735). We have now moved onto a different vision of construction, but Kant gives us no indication that architecture could, to any extent, contribute to its materialisation.

So can architecture only serve philosophy in a propaedeutic way, as a mere grounding metaphor for our future enlightenment? In the last chapter we defended architecture as a medium for 'aesthetic ideas'. These are defined by Kant as:

> representation[s] of the imagination which induce [...] much thought, yet without the possibility of any definite thought, i.e. concept being adequate to [them], and which language consequently can never get quite on level terms with or render *completely intelligible*.
>
> (Kant 1988a, §49)

Architecture was presumably deemed too down-to-earth to communicate the ineffable. Nevertheless we steadfastly stood our ground and hopefully set out the case for proving that architecture too can 'give the imagination a momentum that makes it think more'. It too can 'quicken the mind by opening out for it a view into an immense realm of kindred presentations' (Kant 1988a, §49). Kant's central example of a work of art that expresses an aesthetic idea is a rather mediocre poem by Friedrich the Great:

> Let us part from life without grumbling or regrets
> Leaving the world behind filled with our good deeds ...
>
> (Friedrich the Great cited by Kant 1988a, §49)

Kant suggests that the king is 'animating his rational idea of a cosmopolitan attitude'. He declares that the poem 'spreads in the mind a multitude of *sublime* and calming feelings and a boundless outlook towards a joyful future'. A different feeling for the sublime is emerging here: no longer a rallying call for nature's subjugation, its influence here is 'calming' and propitious to a 'cosmopolitan' frame of mind, whereby one respects and feels at home in the world. Kant then adds the following footnote which reiterates this more refined relation to nature:

> Perhaps nothing more *sublime* has ever been said, or a thought ever been expressed more sublimely than in that inscription above the temple of *Isis* (Mother Nature): 'I am all that is, that was, and that will be and no mortal has lifted my veil'. Segner made use of this idea in an ingenious vignette prefixed to his *Natural Science* so as to first imbue the pupil who he was about to lead into the temple, with the sacred thrill that is meant to attune the mind to solemn attentiveness.
>
> (Kant 1988a, §49)

While not wanting to return to monumental temples, such as the one devoted to the Goddess Isis, as partial embodiments of the sublime, we will re-engage with architecture in the light of these 'sublime' concerns about 'cosmopolitics' and ecology. This different relation to nature will maybe allow us to appreciate its exceedingly dynamic 'forces' with a reduced will to 'power' (§28). We will also bear in mind Kant's earlier injunction, discussed in Chapter 2, not to refuse utopian projects that attempt to realise what 'ought to be' by discussing less conventional, more experimental, forms of architecture.

CHAPTER 5

Building cosmopolitically?

'Fluid geography' and 'total thinking'

It is not really known to us what really man is today, however self-awareness and reason should instruct us on this point; how much more may we err as to what he is to become eventually! Still the soul's thirst reaches out eagerly after these topics so distant from here and strives to find some light in such a dark [field of] knowledge.

(Kant, *Universal Natural History and the Theory of the Heavens*)

Today the vastness, complexity and detail of our knowledge requires restructuring into assimilable wholes, to be imparted even at the most elementary levels in terms of whole systems. We can no longer think in terms of single static entities – one thing, situation, or problem – but only in terms of dynamic changing processes and series of events that interact complexly.

(Buckminster Fuller, 'Emergent Humanity: Its Environment and Education')

In previous chapters we already broached the topic of 'cosmopolitics'. 'Cosmopolitics' can be defined as political thinking which transcends national borders, which attempts to think politics from a global perspective by taking into account the geophysical fact that the earth is a sphere with limited land mass and natural resources.

For Kant the fact that the earth is not endlessly flat engenders, or rather should engender, far-reaching political effects.

We *should* find ways of living together that take into account the reality that large portions of our finite planet consists of mainly uninhabitable 'oceans and deserts'. In his 'Perpetual Peace' essay, already mentioned earlier, he made the radical claim that:

> Since the earth is a globe, humans cannot disperse over an infinite area, but must necessarily tolerate one another's company. And no-one originally has any greater right than anyone else to occupy any particular portion of the earth.
>
> (Kant 1994, 106)

This declaration evidently invites a discussion about property which takes 'particular portion[s] of the earth' together with its resources out of common use sometimes forever with far-reaching effects, but we'll move on ... In Chapter 1 we discussed the importance for Kant of port cities, such as Königsberg, that mediate between the sea and the land, for gaining a sense of the world as an interconnected whole. We saw that, back in the eighteenth century, he had already identified the potential for global technology to create a sense that we are all 'peoples of the [same] earth' with responsibilities toward one another. His hope was that this principled attitude was evolving to the point where 'a violation of rights in *one* part of the world is felt *everywhere*' (Kant 1994, 107–108). We also evoked alternative forms of living, some already existing and some yet to be explored, that complexified his conventional metaphor of the 'dwelling house'. We then contemplated the 'utopian' space that he suggested was potentially opened up by beauty for envisaging a future *sensus communis*. In this chapter we will build on this material, but not in order to produce what Buckminster Fuller called 'solid thinking', but rather to embrace what he meant by 'total thinking' (Buckminster Fuller 1972, 310–328). This more comprehensive way of understanding who we are, or rather *what we might become*, requires us to resituate ourselves within a larger perspective, to measure ourselves in more than just human terms.

The cosmic viewpoint and architecture

Buckminster Fuller (1895–1993) was an engineer, inventor, teacher (e.g. at the Black Mountain College mentioned earlier in relation to architectural practice as a craft). Fuller described himself as a 'comprehensive anticipatory design scientist' (Fuller in Hays and Miller 2008, 62). One might think that Immanuel Kant and Buckminster Fuller are improbable bedfellows. However, in the writings of both the spherical nature of planet Earth within the universe plays an equally central and generative role. For instance, in *Operating Manual for Spaceship Earth*, Buckminster Fuller wrote:

> I've often heard people say, 'I wonder what it would be like to be on board a spaceship', and the answer is very simple. What *does* it feel like? That's all we have ever experienced. We are all astronauts.
>
> (Buckminster Fuller 1976, 42)

Similarly, Kant's *Critique of Practical Reason* culminates in what one might call a most 'sublime' account of how the human should experience himself both as an articulation between this expanding universe situated within a plurality of worlds, and as part of earthly life with all the responsibilities that this complex web of belongingness entails. These 'two things' combined were seen as resonating within the human, enriching his sense of self while depleting his sense of self-importance. The wonder of the 'starry heavens', Kant wrote:

> begins from the place I occupy in the external world of sense, and expands the connection in which I find myself into the incalculable vastness of worlds upon worlds, of systems within systems, over endless ages of their periodic motion, their beginnings and perpetuation.
>
> (Kant 1956, 166)

Kant recalls that we are ultimately stardust ('a mere speck in the universe'), for, as we know, the atomic components (carbon, nitrogen, oxygen, etc.) that make up our bodies were first formed inside the stars (Reeves 1994). We are 'animal-like being[s] who must return [their] matter from whence it came to the planet' (Kant 1956, 166): along with other animals and the plants, we are composed of molecules which have already been recycled many times; the fresh air we inhale has also been 'breathed' many times by other life forms. It is in conjunction with these other life forms that the earth's atmosphere has evolved into something quite different from that surrounding other planets. Such reflection shows the extent to which we as a species interact with other living creatures and with planet Earth. At the same time, Kant evoked an engagement 'independent of animality', one the individual human shares with other 'rational beings', a 'determination' which 'is not restricted to the conditions and limits of this life but radiates into the infinite' (Kant 1956, 166). In its direct appeal to free, autonomous will, this moral law spurs each one of us to activate the sublime 'supersensible substrat of humanity' (Kant 1988a, §57), to project the self beyond the heteronomies of conventional, mediated value. Thus conceived, the moral law enjoins us to appropriate our world, to *act* in this world, using our minds inventively and responsibly, by orienting ourselves towards the future.

The cultivation of different perspectives – the interplanetary (non-geocentrically bound), the inter-supersensory (non-anthropocentrically limited) – was crucial to Kant's cosmopolitical project.

In a similar vein, Buckminster Fuller considered that a less static, more 'fluid' understanding of geography was required to bring about positive change in this evolving world. Contrasting the landsman's static worldview to that of the dynamic sensibility of the sailorman, who is well acquainted with the medium of water, Buckminster Fuller eloquently wrote:

> sailors have come to be the only men of commerce dealing directly and daily with the mechanics of the stars. Confronted with large quantities of unknowns intervening between identified ports, they came early to rely upon instruments and skills of the intellect, upon scientific imaging. In principle 'blind flying' has been employed at sea for centuries. Without thinking of

Ara Güler 'Kumkapi' 1950. The 'cosmic viewpoint' of the sailor.

> themselves as cosmogonists, sailors naturally develop *a cosmic viewpoint. They view the world from outside: they 'come upon' the land.*
>
> (Buckminster Fuller 1972, 133; *my italics*)

A sailor sees universal relations that remain invisible or abstract to the landlubber: 'he "sees" the moon lifting the water as it circles after its rotating and orbiting mother-ship Earth'. His engagement with and navigation of the watery elements of this planet are understood in relation to the stars 'outside' him, not 'above' him as if the stars are 'up there'. The term 'outside' is used designedly by Buckminster Fuller as an essential aspect of his strategy to encourage us to jettison semantic inaccuracies in order to better attune our understanding of the world to our actual experience, and to his vision of the future. He therefore advocates replacing the terms 'up' and 'down' by 'inside' and 'outside'. By so doing he is obliging us to *think through* the spherical nature of the planet as experienced by sailors and adopt their 'cosmic viewpoint'. In an essay entitled 'Total Thinking', he reiterates that:

> If he persists in the up-and-down language man may never communicate accurately with other men for they do not employ the same meanings, either from moment to moment or in respect to their individual ups and downs ... Only when men learn to say in and out relative to designated common centres (for example, of earth) is the meaning constantly reliable. The sky is 'outward' to all men, at all places, at all times, on any planet. While enjoying an infinity of individual 'ins', we, anywhere in the universe, also enjoy one common non-simultaneous, omni-directional aggregate called 'out'.
>
> (Buckminster Fuller 1972, 317–318)

If what we have in common is a 'non-simultaneous, omni-directional aggregate', what are 'we'? As the epigrams to this section indicate, both Kant and Buckminster Fuller thought that us humans have potential that has not yet seen the light. They both hoped that in the future a more 'cosmopolitically' minded humanity would emerge.

<u>For Buckminster Fuller, and Kant, future development</u>

<u>necessitates new ways of thinking about ourselves and our</u>

<u>relation to the world (including the way we build within it).</u>

Tension as a constructive force

In Chapter 2 we saw how, for Kant, the 'unsocial sociability' of humans was not a trait to be eradicated for the sake of a future homogeneous harmony, but instead a source of productive tension (Kant 1994, 44). The negotiation and balancing of antagonistic forces was for him structural to society itself.

Buckminster Fuller holding a tensegrity mast c.1950.

In his *Anthropology*, he offered the following definition of the human collective:

> a multitude of persons existing successively and side by side, who cannot *do without* associating peacefully and yet cannot *avoid* constantly offending one another.
> (Kant 1974a, 191; 1977, 687)

The positivisation of tension was also a major aspect of Buckminster Fuller's rethinking of architecture in terms of what he called 'tensegrity'. The typical 'tensegrity' structure has been defined as follows:

> A spatial truss composed of bars and cables with one bar for at least three cables in each node so that the tension members form a connected set of polygonal lines in space, whereas each of the compression members is isolated.
> (Podio-Guidugli 2011, 271)

Tensegrity structures stabilise themselves through continuous tension and discontinuous compression. They therefore reverse centuries of building tradition that is primarily based on compression, on the gradual amassing of blocks of material (as discussed above in relation to Kant's 'dwelling house', the pyramids and St. Peter's). Buckminster Fuller regards this cumbersome, ecologically unfriendly building method as indicative of antiquated 'solid thinking'. He writes:

> The processes of engineering up to the moment of introduction of my geodesic structures, are predicated on stress analysis of individual beam and column behaviours, as separate components and thereafter upon comprehensively organised beams, columns and cantilevers as a solid compressional overall integrity of cohesion, aided here and there by tensionally exaggerated sinews – tension being subordinate and local.
> (Krause and Lichtenstein 1999, 396)

It is this 'solid thinking' that is overturned by the dynamic fluidity of anticlassical, lightweight tensegrity structures that demonstrate 'associated' rather than 'individual' behaviours, and that prioritise lines of tension over blocks of compression. Tensegrity structures challenge our flat-earth, landlubberish understanding of our environment as they:

> impl[y] a reversal in perception: what appears to be compactly standing and solid proves to be suspended and ephemeral. Tensegrity [is] a philosophical

model of coherence. By what is something held together, then, if not the compact mass? By increasingly thin tensile members that border on the spiritual.

(Krause and Lichtenstein 1999, 396)

Tensegrity structures are presented as fostering a less specialised, more comprehensive way of thinking by putting us more in touch with the universe as a living whole.

Buckminster Fuller's sense of the universalising significance of tensegrity has been corroborated by the cell biologist Donald Ingber, who called it the 'architecture of life'. Ingber wrote:

> An astounding wide variety of natural systems, including carbon atoms, water molecules, proteins, viruses, cells, tissues, and even humans and other living creatures, are constructed using a common form of architecture known as tensegrity.
>
> (Ingber 1998)

Ingber accounts for the ubiquity of tensegrity in nature by placing stress on how the structures stabilise themselves through 'the strength of the entire structure', rather than due to the 'individual strength of individual members'. As such, tensegrity is, he explains:

> the most economical and efficient way to build – at the molecular scale, at the macroscopic scale and at all scales in between. It is possible that fully triangulated tensegrity structures may have been selected through evolution because of their structural efficiency – their high mechanical strength using a minimum of materials. The flexibility exhibited by prestressed tensegrity structures would be advantageous because it allows structures to take on different shapes.
>
> (Ingber 1998)

A tensegrity structure can be flexibly turned into a geodesic dome. Buckminster Fuller explains this conversion process:

> Tensegrity structures are the essence of all geodesic domes. When we increase the frequency of modular subdivisions of geodesic domes the edges of the triangles, representing the chords of central angles, get shorter and shorter and the interval between the mid-chord and the mid-arc of the central angles also decrease with the increasing frequency of the modular subdivision. Because the materials used in the construction of the dome have some substantial dimension, we get to the point where the high-frequency production of the arc-attitude is such that the materials (the individual tensegrity components) touch one another.
> (Buckminster Fuller 1999, 408–409)

Geodesic domes were evoked in Chapter 2 alongside other lightweight mobile constructions, such as tents, in our discussion of alternative, maybe more 'utopian' ways of living. Reminiscent of Kant's vision of his future metaphysical system, a tensegrity-based geodesic dome is 'an organised unity (*articulatio*), and not an aggregate (*coacervatio*)' (Kant 1983, B861). Additionally Buckminster Fuller claims that:

> Because tension and tensegrity have no limit of clear spanning, tensegrity structures open up completely clear spanned domes of any size.
> (Buckminster Fuller 1999, 409)

This 'architecture of life' therefore also 'grow[s] from within (*per intussusceptionem*), not by external addition (*per appositionem*)' as Kant also envisaged (Kant 1983, B861). Tensegrity can be seen as self-adjusting wholes which exhibit collective behaviour which is seemingly not built into individual components in any obvious way. Likewise, the 'sublime' idea of '*cosmopolitics*' should presumably not be considered to be an innate or inherent characteristic of an individual human or amalgamation of humans. It, too, would emerge as a form of collective behaviour that could not be entirely predicted or deliberately produced, though it would be facilitated through changed patterns of social and cultural interactivity.

Buckminster Fuller and his students testing their geodesic dome experiment at Black Mountain College, 1949.

In this chapter we have ended up presenting Immanuel Kant as an astral companion for Buckminster Fuller in the light of their thinking about cosmopolitics.

Maybe the modest 'dwelling house' Kant describes in Critique of Pure Reason, which is parsimonious in its use of building materials, 'just sufficiently roomy for our business on the level of experience, and just sufficiently high to allow of our overlooking it', and which hence demonstrates what Buckminster Fuller calls 'ephemeralisation' ('doing more with less'), could ultimately become a geodesic dome

(Kant 1983, B735; Buckminster Fuller cited by Krausse and Lichtenstein 1999, 16). The stakes involved would be high: it would require a different approach to building practice and a different attitude to the shared life of this planet. As Kant has repeatedly told us, it is incumbent upon us not to resign ourselves to preformatted ways of thinking. We should entertain the 'utopian' prospect of a substantially better future by cultivating a less limited and egotistical, more 'multiperspectival' thinking of ourselves in terms of a global situation (Morgan 2007). Hope is identified by Kant as an important 'spur to action', giving us the forward-driving motivation we need if we are to change the world into a better place (Kant 1956, 152).

Hopeful prospects that might allow a future to emerge, one which is not entirely preconditioned by past events, are often dashed by the depressing effect of so-called 'adverse experience' (Kant 1983, B373). For Kant it was crucial to resist set ideas about, for instance, human nature that often thwart any attempt to aim for many positive changes, such as world peace, by drawing on historical experience for proof that it would never work because so far it never has. This reactive form of thinking is deemed by Kant to be 'vulgar', most 'damaging and not worthy of a philosopher' (Kant 1983, B373; Morgan 2014, 126–129). Following in the wake of Kant's thoughts on architecture, I have been suggesting that this attitude is also not worthy of architects.

Conclusion

Architects of the future unite!

> For many years I have had the intuition that in the world of architecture there lies the possibility of the development of brilliantly educated men [sic] capable of a generalised comprehensive anticipatory science of design, which both can and may be as effective in bringing about man's [sic] general well-being as specialized education has been in bringing about only isolated successes within an otherwise general environment of chaotic dismay, frustration and high-frequency failures.
>
> (Buckminster Fuller, 'The Comprehensive Man' 1959)

We began this book by asking the question 'Why Kant now?' as if he might no longer have anything to say to us. Yet we finished with his injunction that we should bring about change, that there is still a lot to be done.

It is hoped that by actualising Kant's eighteenth-century ideas, by putting his preconceptions of what architecture is and how it relates to the world, together with his cosmopolitical project for the future, our sense of what architecture has been, is now and still could be has been enlivened.

I insisted on how Kant's ideas about critique oblige us to think beyond a prefabricated world into which we just have to fit. He required us to be accountable for our actions. His work on the aesthetic judgement of the beautiful and sublime indicated to us the role architecture could play in creating 'playspace', wherein alternative ways of relating to others become possible.

I emphasised that his work was constantly informed by a concern for the world as an evolving and interconnected whole and how our acts, as particular instances of decision-making, have repercussions within this wider framework. Kant's hope was that such 'cosmopolitical' behaviour would gradually form the 'great political body of the future'. He wrote:

> Although this political body exists for the present only in the roughest of outlines, it nonetheless seems as if a feeling is beginning to stir in all its members, each of which has an interest in maintaining the whole. And this encourages the hope that, after many revolutions, with all their transforming effects, the highest purpose of nature, a universal *cosmopolitan existence*, will at last be realised as the matrix within which all the original capacities of the human race may develop.
>
> (Kant 1994, 51).

In his epic *The Principle of Hope*, Ernst Bloch suggested that hope requires 'people who throw themselves into what is becoming', who 'do not tolerate a dog's life which feels itself only passively thrown into What is' (Bloch 1986, 3). The question I wish to leave you with is:

what would a 'hopeful' theory and practice of architecture, that are equal to Kant's vision, consist of?

My own example has been Buckminster Fuller's tensegrity structures that seem to embody a more collective spirit than conventional edifices. Buckminster Fuller, like Kant, was critical of his age: he thought that the world's problems – such as the shortage of natural resources in many parts of the world – could be solved if only a 'philosophy of fixedness' were to be abandoned and replaced by 'an increasingly dynamic world picture' (Buckminster Fuller 1972, 177). He wrote with urgency about his changed times, as did Kant:

> We can no longer think in terms of the single static entities – one thing, situation, or problem – but only in terms of dynamic changing processes and series of events that interact complexly.
>
> (Fuller 2001, 105)

If we, as thinkers and makers of architecture, are not prepared to accept the existence of a status quo to which we just passively conform, we should take seriously the specific role that architecture plays in our lives and construct the world differently.

Further reading

The main translations I have used for Kant's *Critique of Pure Reason*, *Critique of Practical Reason* and *Critique of Judgement* are those of Kemp Smith, Beck and Meredith respectively (Kant 1983; 1956; 1988b). I have consulted Guyer and Wood's, Gregor's and Pluhar's more recent versions (i.e. Kant 2007; 2008; 1987), and adapted where I deemed it appropriate. I also cite the German original when I felt it was indispensable to do so. In the case of *Critique of Pure Reason* and *Critique of Judgement* I have referred to sections (indicated by the symbol §), rather than pages, so that citations can be found regardless of which edition is being used.

For further background to Kant, his life and work, Manfred Kühn's biography (2001) is very readable. Howard Caygill's *A Kant Dictionary* (1995) is also very helpful, as well as being interesting. He gives the reader a clear sense of why and how Kant uses the terms he does. He also places Kant's ideas in relation to other philosophical figures. John Zammito's *The Genesis of Kant's Critique of Judgement* (1992) gives a detailed account of the context for Kant's thoughts on aesthetic and teleological judgement.

For more on current debates about architecture, specularity and consumer culture, see Foster (2013) and Vidler (2008). For more on architecture and utopian theory and practice, see Dessauce (1999), Busbea (2007), Coleman (2011, 2014a) and Morgan (2008; 2011). The standard work for thinking about ornament as *parergon* is Derrida's *Truth in Painting* (1986), but Antoine Picon's more recent analysis (2013) is specifically tailored to architectural concerns. The architectural metaphor in Kant is analysed in Edelman (1984), Payot (1982) and Morgan (2000). For more on Kant and Buckminster Fuller (as well as Archigram and the importance of space travel), see Morgan

(2013). Kant is presented as an utopian thinker in Morgan (2014). For the interplanetary dimension of Kant's cosmopolitics, see Szendy (2013) and Morgan (2018). Standard works on cosmopolitics include Bohman and Lutz-Bachmann (1997), Cheah and Robbins (1998), Archibugi (2003) and Morgan and Banham (2007).

Bibliography

A.D Architecture Design Profile (1980) *Viollet-le-Duc 1814–1879* (London: Academy Editions).

Adamson, G. (2007) *Thinking Through Craft* (Oxford: Berg).

Archibugi, D. ed. (2003) *Debating Cosmopolitics* (London: Verso).

Augé, M. (2008) *Non-Places: An Introduction to Supermodernity*, trans. J. Howe (London: Verso).

Barthes, R. (1984) *Camera Lucida* (London: Flamingo/Fontana).

Benjamin, W. (1991) 'Neapel' with Asja Lacis in *Gesammelte Schriften*, Vol. IV.I 'Kleine Prosa Baudelaire-Übertragungen' (Franfurt am Main: Suhrkamp).

Benjamin, W. (1996) *Selected Writings*, Vol. I 1913–1926, ed. M. Bullock and M.W. Jennings (Cambridge, MA: Belknap Press Harvard University Press).

Benjamin, W. (1999) *The Arcades Project*, trans. H. Eiland and K. McLaughlin (Cambridge, MA: Belknap Press Harvard University Press).

Benjamin, W. (2002) *Selected Writings*, Vol III 1935–1938, ed. H. Eiland and M.W. Jennings (Cambridge, MA: Belknap Press Harvard University Press).

Beuter, A. and van Hinte, E. (2001) *The Inevitable Renaissance of Minimum Energy Structures* (Rotterdam: Delft University of Technology).

Bloch, E. (1986) *The Principle of Hope*, trans. N. Plaice, S. Plaice and P. Knight, Vol. I (Cambridge, MA: MIT Press).

Bohman, J. and Lutz-Bachmann, M. eds (1997) *Perpetual Peace: Essays on Kant's Cosmopolitan Ideal* (Cambridge, MA: MIT Press).

Buckminster Fuller, R. (1972) *The Buckminster Fuller Reader*, ed. J. Meller (London: Pelican Books).

Buckminster Fuller, R. (1976) *Operating Manual for Spaceship Earth* (New York: Aeonian Press).

Buckminster Fuller, R. (1999) 'Nothing touches anything else', in *Your Private Sky: R. Buckminster Fuller The Art of Design Science*, ed. J. Krause and C. Lichtenstein (Baden: Lar Müller Publishers).

Buckminster Fuller, R. (2001) 'Emergent humanity: its environment and education' in *Anthology for the New Environment*, ed. T.K. Zung (New York: St. Martin's Press).

Burke, E. (1987) *A Philosophical Enquiry into the Origin of our Ideas of the Sublime and Beautiful*, ed. J. Boulton (Oxford: Basil Blackwell).

Busbea, L. (2007) *Topologies: The Urban Utopia in France 1960–1970* (Cambridge, MA: MIT Press).

Carroll, L. (1992) *Alice's Adventures in Wonderland* (New York: William Morrow & Co.).

Caygill, H. (1995) *A Kant Dictionary* (Oxford: Blackwell).

Chadwick, P. (2016) *This Brutal World* (London: Phaidon).

Cheah, P. and Robbins, B., eds (1998) *Cosmopolitics: Thinking and Feeling Beyond the Nation* (Minneapolis, MN: University of Minnesota Press).

Cinqualbre, O. and Migayrou, F. (2015) *Le Corbusier: Mesures de l'homme*, Exhibition Catalogue (Paris: Centre Pompidou).

Clark, W., Golinski, J. and Schaeffer, S. (1999) *The Sciences in Enlightenment Europe* (Chicago, IL: University of Chicago Press).

Coleman, N., ed. (2011) *Imagining and Making the World Reconsidering Architecture and Utopia* (Oxford: Peter Lang).

Coleman, N., ed. (2014a) *Utopian Studies*, Special Issue: Utopia & Architecture Vol. 25, no.1.

Coleman N. (2014b) *Lefebvre for Architects* (Abingdon: Routledge).

Connaissance des arts (2014a) Hors série no. 644 'Frank Gehry' Paris.

Connaissance des arts (2014b) Hors série no. 646 'Fondation Louis Vuitton' Paris.

Cornu, V. (2009) 'In the Thick of Things/Parmi les choses' adapted and trans. D. Gunn (Lewes: Sylph Press).

Crawford, M. (2009) *The Case For Working With Your Hands* (London: Penguin).

Davies, C. (2011) *Thinking About Architecture: An Introduction to Architectural Theory* (London: Laurence King).

Deleuze, G. (1985) *Cinéma 2: L'image temps* (Paris: Les éditions de minuit).

Derrida, J. (1975) 'Economimesis', in *Mimesis des Articulations* (Paris: Aubier-Flammarion).

Derrida, J. (1986) *La vérité en peinture* (Paris: Flammarion).

Dessauce, M., ed. (1999) *The Inflatable Moment: Pneumatics and Protest in '68* (Princeton, NJ: Princeton Architectural Press).

De Zayas, A.-M. (1994) *A Terrible Revenge: The Ethnic Cleansing of the East European Germans 1944–50*, trans. J.A. Koehler (New York: St. Martin's Press).

Edelman, B. (1984) *La maison de Kant* (Paris: Payot).

Elliott, B. (2011) *Benjamin for Architects* (Abingdon: Routledge).

Eze, E.C. (1997) *Race and Enlightenment: A Reader* (Cambridge, MA: Blackwell).

Fondation Louis Vuitton Le Journal (2014), no. 1.

Foster, H. (2013) The Art-Architecture Complex (London: Verso).

Foucault, M (2008) *Introduction to Kant's Anthropology*, ed. R. Nigro, trans. R Nigro and K. Briggs (Los Angeles, CA: Semiotexte).

Goethe, J.W. (1998) 'Maximen und Reflexionen', in *Werke* Hamburger Ausgabe Vol. XIII 'Schriften zur Kunst' (München: Deutscher Taschenbuch Verlag).

Golding, W. (2005) *The Spire* (London: Faber).

Goulyga, A (1985) *Emmanuel Kant: Une Vie*, trans. J.-M. Vaysse (Paris: Aubier).

Hays, K.M. and Miller, D., eds (2008) *Starting With the Universe*, Exhibition Catalogue (New York: Whitney Museum of Modern Art).

Hegel, G.W.F. (1986) *Vorlesungen über die Ästhetik II* in *Werke*, Vol. XIV (Frankfurt am Main: Suhrkamp).

Heidegger, M. (1975) *Poetry, Language, Thought*, trans. and introduction, A. Hofstadter (New York: Harper and Row).

Hocquenghem, G. and Schérer, R. (2013) *L'âme atomique* (Paris: Editions du Sandre).

Hoyle, R. and Pinder, D., eds (1992) *European Port Cities in Transition* (London: Belhaven Press).

Hyde, L. (2006) *The Gift: How the Creative Spirit Transforms the World* (Edinburgh: Canongate Books).

Ingber, D.E. (1998) 'The Architecture of Life', Scientific American. Available online.

Ingber, D.E and Morgan, D. (2001) 'An Interview with Donald Ingber', Culture Machine, Vol. 3. Available online.

Kahn, L. (1991) *Writings, Lectures, Interviews*, ed. A. Latour (New York: Rizzoli).

Kant, I. (1956) *Critique of Practical Reason*, trans. L.W. Beck (New York: Macmillan).

Kant, I. (1974a) *Anthropology from a Pragmatic Point of View*, trans. M. Gregor (The Hague: Martinus Nijhoff).

Kant, I. (1974b) *Kritik der reinen Vernunft*, Werkausgabe Vol. III–IV, ed. W. Weischedel (Frankfurt am Main: Suhrkamp).

Kant, I. (1974c) *Kritik der praktischen Vernunft*, Werkausgabe Vol. VII, ed. W. Weischedel (Frankfurt am Main: Suhrkamp).

Kant, I. (1974d) *Kritik der praktischen Vernunft & Grundlegung zur Metaphysik der Sitten*, Werkausgabe Vol. VI, ed. W. Weischedel (Frankfurt am Main: Suhrkamp).

Kant, I. (1974e) *Kritik der Urteilskraft*, Werkausgabe Vol X, ed. W. Weischedel (Frankfurt am Main: Suhrkamp).

Kant, I. (1977) *Schriften zur Anthropologie, Geschichtsphilosophie, Politik und Pädagogik 2*, Vol. XII, ed. W. Weischedel (Frankfurt am Main: Suhrkamp).

Kant, I. (1983) *Critique of Pure Reason*, trans. N.K. Smith (London: Macmillan).

Kant, I. (1987) *Critique of Judgement*, trans. W.S. Pluhar (Indianapolis, IN: Hackett Publishing Company).

Kant, I. (1988a) *Critique of Judgement*, trans. J.C. Meredith (Oxford: Oxford University Press).

Kant, I. (1988b) 'Prolegomena zu einer jeden künftigen Metaphysk die als Wissenschaft wird auftreten können' in *Schriften zur Metaphysik und Logik*, Werkausgabe Vol. V, ed. W. Weischedel (Frankfurt am Main: Suhrkamp).

Kant, I (1994) *Political Writings*, trans H.B. Nisbet, ed. and notes H. Reiss (Cambridge: Cambridge University Press).

Kant, I. (2007) *Critique of Pure Reason*, trans. P. Guyer and A.W. Wood (Cambridge: Cambridge University Press).

Kant, I. (2008) *Practical Philosophy*, trans. M. Gregor (Cambridge: Cambridge University Press).

Koerner, K.L. (1999) 'Daedalus Hyperborus: Baltic natural history and mineralogy in the enlightenment', in *The Sciences in Enlightened Europe*, ed.W. Clark, J. Golinski and S. Schaeffer (Chicago, IL: University of Chicago Press), pp. 389–422.

Krausse, J. and Lichtenstein, C. (1999) *Your Private Sky: R. Buckminster Fuller, The Art of Design Science* (Frankfurt am Main: Lars Müller Publishers).

Krausse, J. and Lichtenstein, C. (2001) *Your Private Sky: Discourse R. Buckminster Fuller* (Zürich: Lars Müller Publishers).

Kühn, M. (2001) *Kant: A Biography* (Cambridge: Cambridge University Press).

Le Corbusier (1963) *The Modulor: A Harmonious Measure to the Human Scale Universally Applied to Architecture and Mechanics* (London: Faber).

Lefebvre, H. (1991) *The Production of Space*, trans. D. Nicholson-Smith (Oxford: Blackwell Publishing).

Lefebvre, H. (2004) *Rhythmanalysis: Space, Time and Everyday Life*, trans. S Elden and G. Moore (London: Continuum).

Leibniz, G.W. (1969) *Essais de Théodicée* (Paris: Garnier Flammarion).

Lichtenstein C. and Krausse J. (1999) 'How to make the worldwork', in *Your Private Sky: R. Buckminster Fuller The Art of Design Science*, ed. J. Krausse and C. Lichtenstein (Baden: Lar Müller Publishers).

MacGregor, N. (2014) *Germany: Memories of a Nation* (London: Allen Lane/ Penguin).

Marchand, T. and Meffre, R. (2010) *Détroit, vestiges du rêve américain* (Göttingen: Steidl).

Mauss, M. (1985) 'Essai sur le don', in *Sociologie et Anthropologie* (Paris: Presses universitaires de France).

McHale, J.R. (1962) *Buckminster Fuller* (New York: George Braziller).

Migarou, F. (2015) 'Le Modulor Variances d'un invariant', in *Le Corbusier: mesures del'homme*, ed. O. Cinqualbre and F. Migarou, catalogue Georges Pompidou.

Mininger, J.D. and Kant, I. (2005) ' "Nachschrift eines Freundes": Kant, Lithuania and the Praxis of Enlightenment' *Studies in East European Thought*, Vol. 75, no. I, 1–32.

Morgan, D. (2000) *Kant Trouble: The Obscurities of the Enlightened* (London and New York: Routledge).

Morgan, D (2007) 'Kant, Cosmopolitics, Multispectval Thinking and Technology' *Angelaki: Journal of the Theoretical Humanities*, Vol. 12, no. 2, 35–47.

Morgan D. (2008) 'The Distractions the Built Environment: Architecture as a Collective Work of Art', *Interculture*. Available online.

Morgan, D. (2009) 'Trading Hospitality: Kant, Cosmopolitics and *Commercium*', *Paragraph*, Vol. 32, no. I.

Morgan, D. (2011) '*Spielraum* et *Greifbarkeit:* Acheminement vers une architecture utopique', in *Spielraum: W. Benjamin et l'architecture*, ed. L. Andreotti (Paris: Les éditions de la Villette).

Morgan, D. (2013) '"The camel (the ship of the desert)": "Fluid Geography", "Globality", Cosmopolitics in the Work of Immanuel Kant', in *The Epistemology of Utopia: Rhetoric, Theory and Imagination*, ed. J. Bastos da Silva (Newcastle Upon Tyne: Cambridge Scholars Publishing).

Morgan, D. (2014) '*Globus terraqueus* Cosmopolitan Law and "Fluid Geography" in the Utopian Thinking of Immanuel Kant and Pierre-Joseph Proudhon', in *Law and the Utopian Imagination*, ed. A. Sarat, L. Douglas and M.M. Umphrey (Stanford, CA: Stanford University Press).

Morgan, D. (2018) *Kant, Cosmopolitics and Globality* (Basingstoke: Palgrave Macmillan).

Morgan, D. and Banham, G., eds (2007) *Cosmopolitics and the Emergence of the Future* (Basingstoke: Palgrave Macmillan).

Motro, R. and Podio-Guidugli (2003) *Tenségrité: analyse et projets – Revue française de génie civile* (Paris: Lavoisier).

Mumford, L. (1940) *The Culture of Cities* (London: Secker & Warburg).

Nietzsche, F. (1987) *Untimely Meditations*, trans. R.J. Hollingdale (Cambridge: Cambridge University Press).

Nietzsche, F. (1968) *The Will to Power*, trans. W. Kaufman (New York: Vintage).

Nietzsche, F. (1990) *Twilight of the Idols/The Anti-Christ*, trans. R.J. Hollingdale (Harmondsworth: Penguin).

Nye, D.E. (1994) *American Technological Sublime* (Cambridge MA: MIT Press).

Odey, J. (2014) 'Chef d'œuvres en lumière', Polka, Vol. 28.

Otto, F. (1982) *Natürliche Konstruktionen* (Stuttgart: Deutsche Verlags-Anstalt).

Podio-Guidugli, P. (2011) 'The Tensegrity Arch at TorVergata: A gateway to the university campus and a full-scale experimental facility', *Tenségrité: analyse et projets*, Vol. 7, 263–273.

Payot, D. (1982) *Le philosophe et l'architecte* (Paris: Aubier Montaigne).

Phillips, C. (1989) *Photography in the Modern Era: European Documents and Critical Writings 1913–1940* (New York: The Metropolitan Museum of Modern Art/Aperture).

Picon, A. (2013) *Ornament: The Politics of Architecture and Subjectivity* (Chichester: John Wiley & Sons).

Reeves, H. (1994) *Poussière d'étoiles* (Paris: Les éditions du seuil).

Rodchencko, A. (1989) 'The paths of modern photography' in *Photography in the Modern Era: European Documents and Critical Writings 1913–1940*, ed. C. Phillips (New York: The Metropolitan Museum of Art/Aperture).

Rudofsky, B. (1964) *Architecture Without Architects* (London: Academy Editions).

Ruskin, J. (1988) *The Seven Lamps of Architecture*, introduction by A. Saint (London: National Trust Classics/Century Hutchinson Ltd).

Ruskin, J. (2011) *The Nature of Gothic*, preface by W. Morris, facsimile of the Kelmscott edition (London: Pallas Athene).

Sachs, W. (2010) 'One World', in *The Development Dictionary*, ed. W. Sachs (Huntington: Zed Books).

Schiller, F. (1982) *On the Aesthetic Education of Man*, bilingual edition, trans. E.M. Wilkinson and L.A. Willoughby (Oxford: Clarendon Press/Oxford University Press).

Sharr, A. (2007) *Heidegger for Architects* (Abingdon: Routledge).

Summerson, J. (1980) 'Viollet-le-Duc and the rational point of view', in *Architectural Design Profile: Viollet-le-Duc* (London: Academy Editions), p. 11.

Swift, J. (1982) *Gulliver's Travels* (Harmondworth: Penguin).

Szendy, P. (2013) *Kant in the Land of Extraterrestrials: Cosmopolitical Philosofictions*, trans. W. Bishop (New York: Fordham University Press).

Thompson, D'Arcy (1961) *On Growth and Form* (Cambridge: Cambridge University Press).

Vaudeville, B. (1999) 'The Folly of Structures: An Apology for Rigidity', trans. D. Morgan in *Tekhnema*, Vol. 5.

Vidler, A. (2008) *Architecture Between Spectacle and Use* (Williamstone, MA: Sterling and Francine Clark Institute).

Violeau, X. (1999) 'Utopie: in acts', in *The Inflatable Moment: Pneumatics and Protest in '68*, ed. M. Dessauce (Princeton, NJ: Princeton Architectural Press).

Viollet- le- Duc, E.E. (1856) *Description de Notre-Dame Cathédrale de Paris* (Paris: Librairie d'architecture de France), facsimile.

Viollet-le-Duc, E.E. (1986) *Entretiens sur l'architecture* (Paris: Pierre Mardaga).

Vitruve (1979) *Les dix livres d'architecture*, corrected and trans. C. Perrault (Bruxelles: Pierre Mardaga).

Vitruvius (1960) *The Ten Books on Architecture*, trans. M.H. Morgan (New York: Dover Publications Inc.).

Wölfflin, H. (1950) *The Principles of Art History: The Problem of the Development of Style in Later Art* (New York: Dover Publications).

Wölfflin, H. (2009) *Renaissance und Barock: Eine Untersuchung über Wesen und Entstehung des Barockstils in Italien* (Basel: Schwabe Verlag).

Zammito, J. (1992) *The Genesis of Kant's Critique of Judgement* (Chicago, IL: University of Chicago Press).

Zammito, J. (2002) *Kant, Herder, the Birth of Anthropology* (Chicago, IL: University of Chicago Press).

Zung, T.T.K., ed. (2001) *Buckminster Fuller: Anthology for the New Millennium* (New York: St Martin's Press).

Index

Adamson, G. 55–56
aesthetic ideas 81–82, 84, 89–90, 93, 111
aesthetic judgement, concept of 10, 63, 66, 71–75, 88, 90, 95–96, 103, 125
agreeableness 64, 70, 77, 95
agriculture 77, 93
'anonymous' architecture 37
Anthropology from a Pragmatic Point of View 13–16, 119
Archigram 40
architects 6, 8–9, 17, 22–23, 44, 46, 51, 56–57, 79, 124–25; political responsibilities of 17; *see also* professional architects
architectural projects 33–34, 46, 51
architecture 1–5, 8–11, 18, 20, 23–97, 100–105, 107–9, 111–12, 120–121, 124–27; anonymous 37; communal 40; contemporary 39, 80; integrated 18; and its relation to beauty 48–88; mobile 40; nonpedigreed 23, 39; 'precarious situation of' 48–87; role in Kant's presentation of the sublime 10, 125; and sculpture 37, 85
Architecture without Architects 23, 39

Arnault, Bernard 60–62
art forms 6, 9, 34–35, 48, 51, 81–82, 87, 90, 103–4, 107; liberal 50; subordinate 50; subsidiary 10
Aubert, Jean 40
autonomy 5, 30, 67, 74–75, 77, 82

Babel, Tower of 36, 42–43, 45
ballooning 25, 27
Baltiisk (port) 20
Baroque style 84–85
'basic measure' (unit of assessment) 100–102
'beautiful form' 81, 84
beauty 1–3, 48–50, 57, 59, 65–72, 75–77, 79, 81, 85, 88–89; building's 67; dependent 59; genuine 81, 89; musical 89; natural 89; pure 87, 89; *see also* 'free beauty'
Benjamin, Walter 3–4, 6–9, 33–34, 43, 52
Benjaminian *flâneur* 12
Bilbao 22–23
Bilbao Guggenheim 62
Black Mountain College 55, 114, 123
Bloch, Ernst 126
botanists 71–72
'Building, Dwelling, Thinking' (essay) 5

building materials 43, 46, 123
building sites 16, 43–46, 51–52, 54, 57
buildings 3–4, 34–34, 37, 39, 45, 75, 77–78, 81–82, 86–87, 108–9; abuse of 35; beautiful 60
Burke, Edmund 96

calculation 101–2
capacity 36, 39, 74–75, 78, 92–93, 97, 108
capitalism 3–4, 12, 27, 60
Carroll, Lewis 98
caryatids 81–84
The Case for Working With Your Hands 53
charms 76–79, 81, 85, 90
citizens 12–15, 19, 23, 29, 60
'citizens of the world' 12–15, 19, 23, 29, 60
Coleman, N. 3
colorisation 78–79
colour 78–80; in architecture in Kant's world 78; can 'be considered beauties' (Kant) 78; obfuscates the shape of buildings and heightens the illusion of their movement 78; sympton of 'crude and uncultivated taste' (Kant) 79; and the use of in the 'Brutalist' Park Hill estate 79; 'vibrations *pulsus* of the ether in uniform temporal sequence' (Kant) 78
commercialism 39
commodity culture 10
comprehension, concept of 102–3, 105

concepts 47–49, 64–65, 74, 76, 81, 83, 86, 90, 107, 111; animating 50; guiding 40; narrow 39; numerical 101
Connaissances des arts 62, 69
construction 8, 10, 33, 39, 51–53, 56–57, 67, 111, 122; creative 8; process 17; sites 43; temporary 41; workers 44
consumer 22, 56–60, 66; 'culture' 7, 58; markets 22
corporatised spaces 2
cosmic viewpoint 114, 117–18
cosmopolitan 15, 17, 25, 28, 42, 112, 126
cosmopolitical 95–112; behaviour 126; citizens 20; development 15; differences 33; engagement 13; projects 40, 43, 116, 125
cosmopolitics 10, 20, 28, 108, 112–13, 122–23
country dances 49
craft 51, 53–56, 61, 69, 102, 115; as a type of sub-'art' *Lohnkunst* 51, 53
craftsmanship 53–56, 61
Crawford, Matthew 53–54, 102
critical projects 8, 11, 24–47, 57, 110
critique 36, 42, 51, 57, 63, 87, 90, 93, 95–96, 100; implicit 88; Kant's notion of 10, 24, 27–28, 125
Critique of Judgment 10, 51, 57, 63–64, 87, 90, 95
Critique of Practical Reason 115
Critique of Pure Reason 24, 36, 42, 100, 109, 123

culture 7, 36, 40, 42, 46, 57–58, 71, 75, 87–88, 98; ancient Mediterranean 21; consumer 56, 59–60; visual 4, 7, 77

dance 43, 84, 110
Deleuze, G. 4
dependent beauty 59
Derrida, Jacques 85, 88
design 57, 101
determinant 72, 95
determinant judgement 75
'determining form' 84
disinterest 65–67, 73–74, 95
Douiret 37–39
'dwelling house' (Kant) 36, 43, 109, 111, 114, 120
dwelling houses 46, 57; see also houses

earth 5, 10, 25–26, 42, 62, 108, 113–14, 118
ecological 37, 59; composition 9; dwellings 37
ecology 10, 108, 112
edifice, concept of 36–37, 47, 51, 57, 59, 63, 84, 87, 104–5, 126
Eiffel Tower 103
engineering 120
engineers 51, 71, 83, 114
Enlightenment 7, 16, 27, 30
ephemeralisation 123
experimental involvement 95
eyes 9, 50, 70, 87, 92, 102–3; of others 89; our own 77

films 4, 20, 43
finery 81, 87; distinguished by Kant from 'ornament' 81, 85; mars 'genuine beauty' 81; used to impress 'the eyes of others' (Kant) 89
firmitas ('durability of architecture') 1–3, 48
flâneur 12
flexible 4–5, 37, 101, 109
'fluid geography' 113
Fourier, Charles 4, 15
'free beauty' 58–59, 71, 86, 100
Fuller, Buckminster 11, 84, 113–26; functionality 1, 5, 10, 48, 50, 58, 100
'furtherance of life' 68, 94

Gehry, Frank 10, 23, 33, 56–57, 60, 62, 101
geodesic domes 122–23
gift, the 68
global 2–4, 7, 13–14, 19, 22–23, 26–27, 60, 108, 113–14, 124
global communication networks 18
Goethe 30
good (the) 64
Greene, David 40, 41
Grenzen (limits) 30–33, 110

Haines, Pat 41
happiness, 'conjures up a sensual well-being' (Kant) 62–3
haptic 35
Heidegger, Martin 3, 5–6, 8
Herron, Ron 40

Hirschhorn, Thomas 26
home 10, 17, 35–36, 41, 91, 97, 103, 112
homogenising production of space 7
hope 25
hopeful 126
horticulture 77
houses 5, 35–37, 40–42, 57, 69, 77, 92, 98
Hyde, Lewis 68

as if it were an objective judgement 71
as if it were an objective quality 71
imagination 1–2, 85, 89, 97, 99–103, 106, 111; and intuition 105; popular 52; and understanding 3
inadequacy 97, 103–4, 106; effects of due to 'excessive' proximity (Kant) 104; of the imagination 103
Ingber, D.E. 121
intention 8–9, 11, 25, 50–52, 67, 69, 83, 87
interest 47, 62, 64–65, 67–68, 76, 79, 89, 97, 126; of the agreeable and the good separated from the beautiful 64; of Immanuel Kant's architecturally related ideas 8; to invest in the spatial quality 8; in recent re-evaluations of 'craft' 54
intuition 48, 100–102, 105–7, 111, 125

Jencks, Charles 56
judgement 51, 63, 65, 68, 71–72, 74, 77–78, 93, 95, 97–98; determinant 75; matured 27; reflective 74–75; subjective 70–71; of taste 68, 70, 72
judgment 64, 71–73

Kahn, Louis 91
Kaliningrad 20–23, 57
Kant, Immanuel 1, 4, 8, 87, 123, 125; analysis of the criterion of beauty 10, 29, 57, 67, 81, 92; analysis of the notion of 'the good' 10; *Anthropology from a Pragmatic Point of View* 13; argues that beauty creates a space for freedom 65; association of architecture with 'use' 83; attributes characteristics of prudence and vigilance to architecture 46; and Buckminster Fuller 115, 118; cosmopolitical thinking 109; critical projects 8, 11, 24–47, 57, 110; and the *Critique of Practical Reason* 115; and the *Critique of Pure Reason* 24, 36, 42, 100, 109, 123; definition of architecture 84; and the differences between our world and that of 3, 7, 10, 78; distinguishes between our limits *Grenzen* and our limitations *Schranken* 30–32, 73, 106; and the dynamic world 4, 8; and his assumptions about what constitutes a modest 'dwelling house' 109; and his cosmopolitical thinking 109; and his discussion on 'ornament' 80; and his 'sublime' cosmopolitical future 11; and his term 'mercenary art' 53,

72, 82, 86, 102; and his views on
enlightenment 7, 16, 24, 27, 30,
111; and his vision of what form his
cosmopolitical future might take 11;
ideas 6, 125; image of architecture
56; life history 12, 19; rebukes cynics
25; reckons music has a certain lack
of urbanity about it 93; reference
to the Tower of Babel 43; revisits
the biblical story from *Genesis* 42;
a rigorously ethical thinker 58; and
the significance of Königsberg in his
writings on cosmopolitics 10; stresses
the need to synthesise an in-depth
immersion in our local, regional and
national culture 14; and his 'sublime'
cosmopolitical' project 40; vision of
his future metaphysical system 122
knowledge 10, 13–14, 18–19, 23–24,
36, 46, 55, 71–72, 111, 113; basic
73; expert 9; human 92, 110; a mere
aggregate of 109
Königsberg 10, 12–13, 15–20, 23, 57,
78, 104, 114
Kühn, M. 19

La Fondation Louis Vuitton 10, 33, 44–
45, 57, 59–60, 62, 67–68, 77, 94
labour 12, 62–63
landlubber 25, 120
Le Corbusier 101
Lefebvre, Henri 3, 6–8, 12, 51, 77
liberty 61, 91, 103–4; public 98
Lichtenstein 120–121, 124

life forms 115–16
light 5, 7, 49, 85, 91, 109, 112–13,
118, 123
limitations *Schranken* 30–32, 74, 106
limits *Grenzen* 30–33, 110
Lithuanian culture 16, 20, 22
Lohnkunst ('mercenary'art) 51
LVMH 60–61; *see also* Louis Vuitton
Moët Hennessey
Lynn, Jack 79

Marchand, Yves 60
materials 1, 33, 36–37, 42, 55, 69,
79, 114, 120–122; piled-up 110;
redundant 33; transform 100
Matmata, Tunisia 37–38
Mauss, Marcel 68
measure 76, 91, 98–102, 108, 114
measurement 98–99
'mercenary art' 51, 53
Mininger, J.D. 16
mobile 7, 12, 40, 109, 122
modernists 6
modular subdivisions 122
Modulor, notion of (Le Corbusier) 101
monoculture 2
monuments 23, 59, 102–4, 108–9
Morgan, D. 6–7, 25, 27–28, 33–34, 124
Morris, William 62–63, 67
multiculturalism 15, 18
Mumford, Lewis 108–9
museums 61, 92
music 43, 50, 59, 86, 90, 92–93
musical festivals 41

Naples 4
nature 24–25, 27, 57, 59, 71, 79, 81, 83–84, 107–9, 112; human 31–32, 124; inner 72; intrinsic 31; spherical 115, 117; ungraspable 76; untamed 85; wild 107
The Nature of the Gothic 62
Nietzsche, Friedrich 19

objects 49, 64–65, 67–72, 74, 76–80, 83, 100, 102, 106–7, 111; aesthetic 90; artistic 82; beautiful 75; for sensation 78
Operating Manual for Spaceship Earth 115
'ornament,' Kant's notion of 48, 63, 80–81, 85, 87

parergon 48, 80
Paris 57, 60, 83, 88
perpetual peace 25, 27, 108, 114
photographs 43, 60
photography 71
Picon, A. 78, 86–87
Pinder, D. 21–22
planet 8, 19–20, 25, 27, 29, 54, 62, 108, 118, 124; finite 113; spherical 13
planet Earth 115–16
Plato 32
'play of nature' 15
playroom *Spielraum* 33–34
'playspaces' 34, 50, 59, 125
poetry 50, 89–92

Poland 20, 22
political thinking 113
port cities 14, 23, 114; integrated 21; post-industrial 22
ports 15, 20–22, 116
powers 3, 16, 24, 28, 31–32, 46, 60–61, 99, 107, 112; cognitive 90; mental 93; technological 108
'prefabricated' world (Kant) 6, 125
professional architects 8, 56
purpose 5, 33, 48, 53, 59, 83, 85–87, 103, 107, 110; highest 126; identifiable utilitarian 34; natural 71; particular 69;
'purposiveness without purpose' (beauty) 49
pyramids 102–5, 107–8, 111, 120; a 'mass of dead buildings' (Lewis Mumford) 108

reason 24, 26–29, 35, 55, 64, 84, 98, 100, 104–6, 113; collective 73; force of 105; human 24, 32, 47; nature of 24; powers of 28; speculative 36
reflective judgement 74–75
regularity 12, 48, 85, 88
representation 3, 49, 65–68, 73, 80, 100, 102, 107, 111
responsibilities 1, 24, 47, 114–15; moral 10; political 17, 59
responsible actants 13
River Pregel 13
Rodchenko, Alexander 103
Rudofsky, Bernard 23, 37, 39–40, 45

Ruskin, John 62–63, 67
Russian Federation 20, 22

sailors 116–18
Schranken, (limitations) 30–32, 74, 106
sculpture 35, 43, 55, 77, 81–85, 103–4; and architecture 82, 84; figures 84
Second World War 20
self-knowledge 27
sensation 64–65, 67, 77–79, 95
*sensus comm*unis (common sense) 73, 95, 114
The Seven Lamps of Architecture 63
signature architects 23
societies 6, 21, 54, 66, 118
solidity 1–2, 5, 33, 47, 51, 100
spaces 1–4, 6–7, 13–14, 18, 63, 65, 70, 72, 74, 109; beautiful 3, 34; closeted 41; empty 32; enclosed 4; inclusive 72; interior 37, 104; physical 69; private 19; public 4; utopian 74, 114
Spaceship Earth 115
spectacle 58, 60, 87
Spielraum 33–34
St. Peter's Basilica 103–6, 108, 111, 120
standardisation 60, 99
'starchitect' 23, 57
Statue of Liberty 103–4
statues 81–82
Stinco, Antoine 40
structures 23, 33, 35, 37, 47, 71, 79, 84, 121, 126; geodesic 120; lightweight 84; mobile 109; portable 41; speculative 32, 47; temporary 1; tensegral 84
subcontract 16–17, 46
sublime 3, 10, 40, 74, 95–112, 115–16, 122, 125; experience 74, 100, 104; images 60; sculptural ruin 35
sublime destabilises us 97
Sugar Islands 16
Summerson, John 92
'supersensible substrat of humanity' 116
sustainability 40, 80
sustainable development 10
Swift, Jonathan 98
systems 37, 110, 113, 115; art of constructing 109; class 59; metaphysical 122; natural 121; philosophical 2, 36, 46, 109

taste 2, 65, 67–68, 70–77; acquired 61; aesthetic 77, 80, 85; buds 75; classical 85; crude and uncultivated 79; to judge 71
technological developments 22, 99
technologised times 53
technology 7, 10, 18, 21, 25, 33, 102, 107–8; digital 53, 78; global 23, 114; maritime 22; mobile 7; modern 7
tensegrity structures 120–122; lightweight 120; prestressed 121; stabilising themselves through continuous tension and discontinuous compression 120; triangulated 121
tensile 121
tension 118, 120, 122

theatre 50
thinkers 1, 3, 6, 8–9, 29, 58;
   of architecture 3, 18, 20, 95;
   contemporary 3; critical 3; Henri
   Lefebvre 3, 6–8, 12, 51, 77; and
   makers of architecture 127; and
   Martin Heidegger 3, 5–6, 8; and
   Walter Benjamin 3–4, 6–9, 12,
   33–34, 43, 52
thinking 5, 7–10, 17, 19, 97, 99, 110,
   116, 118, 123–24; solid 114, 120;
   total 113–14, 118
Thinking About Architecture 9
tourism 18, 39
Tower of Babel 36, 42–43, 45
travel 13–15, 109
travellers 18
Triple E ships 22
troglodytes 37–39, 109
Tunisia 37–38

urbanity 13, 90, 92–93
usefulness 1, 28, 31, 33, 35, 48, 50

utilitas in architecture 1–3, 33, 48–50
utopian 5, 10, 25, 55, 59–61,
   122, 124
utopian projects 27, 32, 34, 40–41,
   59, 62, 66, 68, 87, 95
utopianism 32, 95

venustas 1–3, 48
visual 4, 7, 34, 49, 56, 77, 85, 90, 92,
   100; the 77, 90, 92
visual arts 34, 77, 90, 92
visual culture 4, 7, 77
visualization 7, 100
Vitruvius 1–3, 33

'wallpaperisation' 80, 85, 87–88
wallpapers 59, 86
Webb, Michael 41
'The Work of Art in the Age of Its
   Technological Reproducibility' 4
workers 43–44, 53, 63; migrant 17,
   41; subcontracted to the building
   site 16

Taylor & Francis eBooks

Helping you to choose the right eBooks for your Library

Add Routledge titles to your library's digital collection today. Taylor and Francis ebooks contains over 50,000 titles in the Humanities, Social Sciences, Behavioural Sciences, Built Environment and Law.

Choose from a range of subject packages or create your own!

Benefits for you
- Free MARC records
- COUNTER-compliant usage statistics
- Flexible purchase and pricing options
- All titles DRM-free.

Benefits for your user
- Off-site, anytime access via Athens or referring URL
- Print or copy pages or chapters
- Full content search
- Bookmark, highlight and annotate text
- Access to thousands of pages of quality research at the click of a button.

 Free Trials Available We offer free trials to qualifying academic, corporate and government customers.

eCollections – Choose from over 30 subject eCollections, including:

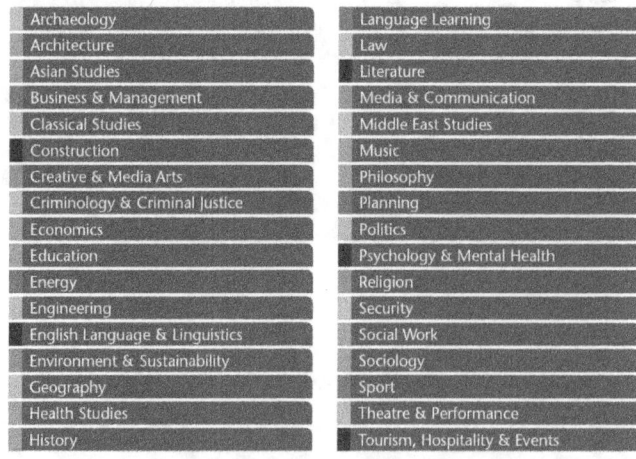

Archaeology	Language Learning
Architecture	Law
Asian Studies	Literature
Business & Management	Media & Communication
Classical Studies	Middle East Studies
Construction	Music
Creative & Media Arts	Philosophy
Criminology & Criminal Justice	Planning
Economics	Politics
Education	Psychology & Mental Health
Energy	Religion
Engineering	Security
English Language & Linguistics	Social Work
Environment & Sustainability	Sociology
Geography	Sport
Health Studies	Theatre & Performance
History	Tourism, Hospitality & Events

For more information, pricing enquiries or to order a free trial, please contact your local sales team:
www.tandfebooks.com/page/sales

 | The home of Routledge books

www.tandfebooks.com

For Product Safety Concerns and Information please contact our EU representative GPSR@taylorandfrancis.com
Taylor & Francis Verlag GmbH, Kaufingerstraße 24, 80331 München, Germany

www.ingramcontent.com/pod-product-compliance
Lightning Source LLC
Chambersburg PA
CBHW070309230426
43664CB00015B/2701